HEALING
HEARTS

A Journey in the Midst of
Spiritual Adversity

Kathy Shelton

WESTBOW°
PRESS
A DIVISION OF THOMAS NELSON
& ZONDERVAN

Cover photo taken by Kathy Shelton in Ouray, Colorado.

Scripture taken from the New King James Version ®. Copyright © 1982
by Thomas Nelson, Inc. Used by permission. All rights reserved.

The principles outlined in this book are not a substitute for therapy.
Persons who display severe emotional symptoms are encouraged to seek
the help of a competent, Christian, mental health professional.

WestBow Press books may be ordered through booksellers or by contacting:

WestBow Press
A Division of Thomas Nelson & Zondervan
1663 Liberty Drive
Bloomington, IN 47403
www.westbowpress.com
1 (866) 928-1240

ISBN: 978-1-4908-2471-0 (sc)
ISBN: 978-1-4908-2473-4 (hc)
ISBN: 978-1-4908-2472-7 (e)

Library of Congress Control Number: 2014901757

Printed in the United States of America.

WestBow Press rev. date: 01/31/2014

Dedication

Without a doubt, since 1986, the most important influence in my life has been my Lord and Savior, Jesus Christ. This book is not only dedicated to Him, but without Him, it would not have been possible. I will never be able to thank God enough for what He has done for me and in me.

In addition, I dedicate this book to my mother, Dorothy Dunlop, who went to be with the Lord on July 20, 2005. My mom invited Jesus into her heart after I was miraculously healed of an incurable disease. She died of cancer, but her faith never once faltered as her illness progressed. I *praise God* that my mother is with Jesus in heaven. I know she would be extremely excited about this book.

Acknowledgments

I am very grateful to Donna Maull, my precious "sister," who assisted in the birthing of this book by proofreading and editing it for me. Her encouragement and suggestions were greatly appreciated and priceless.

To all those that the Lord has put in my life throughout the years, I also say, "Thank you." Each one of you has helped me learn, grow, and trust God in various ways. There are too many to thank individually, but you know who you are. I pray that God blesses you abundantly.

Contents

Introduction

For many years, the Lord has been preparing me to write this book. He has been the guiding force in my life since October 16, 1986, when I asked Jesus Christ to be my Lord and Savior. I had no idea at the time all that would entail, but I have never regretted that life-changing decision. Being an author is not something I ever desired to do, but I know that this *is* the Lord's will. I also know that what the Lord directs, He blesses.

Therefore, I am blessed to convey what is in my heart about the journey the Lord has had me on during the past twenty-seven years. It has been joyful and sad, exhilarating and exhausting, inspiring and heartbreaking, and much more. Along this journey, I have been made increasingly aware that the following verse is undeniably true.

> *And we know that all things work together for good*
> *to those who love God, to those who are the called*
> *according to His purpose.*
>
> (Romans 8:28)

Never have I been more convinced than I am now, that God uses everything in our lives for good. I have lived through significant pain and trauma and have prayed with many who have also survived the full gamut of trauma and are now living very productive lives in the freedom that only Jesus Christ can provide.

Healing Hearts: A Journey in the Midst of Spiritual Adversity is the account of many of my personal experiences as well as what the Lord has taught me through others over the years. I am not a physician although I do have some training and experience working in the medical field. At one time, I was an Associate Member of the *American Academy of Environmental Medicine*. I am also not a licensed counselor, psychologist, psychiatrist, or in any way part of the secular mental health profession.

I am an ordained minister who leads hurting people into freedom with inner healing prayer, and I have witnessed phenomenal results through the healing power of Jesus Christ. Jesus is the Way, the Truth, and the Life! His love and compassion have grown in my heart as my journey has taken numerous twists and turns. Without Jesus' sacrifice and His love, I do not believe healing of deep emotional and spiritual wounds would be possible.

If Jesus is your Lord and Savior, I pray that this book will encourage and bless you. If you do not yet know Jesus as your personal Lord and Savior, I pray that reading this book will draw you into that relationship and that your life will never be the same.

Kathy Shelton
Cofounder, *All for Jesus Ministries*

Chapter One

New York to New Mexico

That's right. It all began in New York. I was born in Queens, one of the five boroughs of New York City. The journey to New Mexico, where I now live with my husband of more than thirty years, began over forty years ago. Every part of my life, including the things that occurred before my relationship with Jesus Christ became a reality, has contributed to my ability to have compassion for those with broken hearts.

I was raised Catholic, attended Catholic school until the middle of sixth grade, and went through all of the traditional milestones in the faith, such as baptism as a baby, First Communion, and confirmation. However, although they exposed me to the existence of God and His Son, Jesus Christ, none of that brought me into a personal relationship with Jesus. Only after I made a deeply heart-felt profession of faith and invited Jesus Christ into my life in 1986 was I able to begin my journey of becoming yielded to God. That made all the difference and paved the way for the Lord to work miracles in and through me.

On that wonderfully fateful evening in October 1986, a dear friend, Janet, and her husband, Rick, the pastor of a Baptist church, visited my husband and me at our home. We had gone to their church after I worked with Janet for a while at a doctor's office where she was the nurse. Janet had no transportation during her lunch breaks, but she often got a ride to the homes of people who were ill or unable for another reason to come to church. I gave Janet a ride to those homes several times and watched in awe as this godly woman loved the people the way Jesus taught—by reading the Bible out loud and praying with them. I had never before witnessed such sacrificial love. I wanted to experience what was causing her to live like that. Her genuine love for people is what sparked my interest to check out their church.

My life changed forever the night Pastor Rick and Janet led me in a prayer to begin my personal relationship with Jesus. Bob had accepted Jesus as a child, but he was definitely not walking with the Lord at that time. Before that night, I was living for myself, doing whatever pleased me and much of it resulted in emotional pain and trauma. I was not attending church anywhere as I had decided that God and the whole religion thing were a farce. I was very cynical and even doubted much of what I had been taught growing up. It was only by the grace of God that I did not end up in serious trouble or dead. *Thank God*, He showered me with His mercy over and over. I believe that His hand was always upon my life in spite of my rebellion and lack of faith.

Please don't misunderstand me. I was a good kid. I applied myself in school, receiving straight A's and a place in the National Honor Society. My proper behavior while living at home was partly because my father was extremely strict. I enjoyed learning and studied hard to receive good grades. Nevertheless, I also knew that doing otherwise could result in dire consequences for me. My father loved me, and I never doubted that. I now understand that he tried to make up for having to work the graveyard shift and for sleeping during the day by keeping an iron hand on my sister and me. He sometimes went over the line of discipline into physical abuse, but we learned quickly how to avoid getting into those situations.

As a result of my diligent school work and excellent grades, I was also awarded a four-year academic scholarship to St. John's University in New York. I was overjoyed! I had applied myself and was going to reap the benefits of all that hard work.

However, one of the very emotionally difficult choices I had to make in my life was when my parents, a week before I was to start college in September 1971, informed me they had decided to move to New Mexico as soon as possible. We had visited Albuquerque on a cross-country driving vacation in the summer of 1969, and they had purchased a small piece of property there. Now my father, who often struggled with depression and insomnia, was at the end of his rope and needed to make this move for his health and sanity. Understanding the reasons for their decision did not make things any easier for me. My plans to become a math teacher were coming apart at the seams.

Another emotional blow came when my extended family in the area, with whom I had planned to live in exchange for babysitting, changed their minds because my parents would be over two thousand miles away in New Mexico. I was eighteen years old and would have had to get a full-time job to pay for my living expenses. I was torn between this amazing educational opportunity and being close to my parents and sister. In just a matter of days, I made the heart-wrenching choice to let the scholarship go and moved to New Mexico with my parents and sister.

Once in New Mexico, I found a job in order to start saving money for college. I was offered partial scholarships at the University of New Mexico and the College of Albuquerque, but neither my parents nor I had any money for the rest of the tuition. Also, I was now a nonresident, having recently moved from New York, so tuition was much higher. I had no choice except to work until I could establish residency status.

In the summer of 1972, I got engaged to Al (not his real name). We were very much in love. Not long before we were going to be married, Al's brain tumor, which had been dormant for years, began growing, causing him terrible headaches and blackouts. His parents took him to a medical facility in another state, where he underwent brain surgery to remove a portion of the tumor. Al's parents did not discuss anything with me about his condition. They left me completely in the dark. All I received were vague answers in response to my questions about his illness and future medical treatment.

When they returned home, Al was not the same person. While I was visiting him at his parents' home one evening, he broke off our engagement. I received no explanation other than that it was not a good time for him to be engaged. My heart broke into a million pieces. I was devastated.

A few days later, on Christmas Eve, as I attended midnight Mass with my parents and sister, all I could do was cry. I sobbed on the way to church, throughout the service, and all the way home. I will never forget the intensity of that pain, although the Lord has since healed my heart. At the time, I responded to the pain by blaming God and rebelling against Him. That did not work out well at all.

About a month after that traumatic experience, I moved out of my parents' home into an apartment, and my behavior quickly deteriorated. I started keeping company with less than godly people. My friends definitely affected how I was living. The Bible states in 1 Corinthians 15:33, "Do not be deceived: Evil company corrupts good habits." This was certainly true in my life. There were numerous times, too many to count, when I got myself into ridiculous and often dangerous situations that I wish had never happened. I am certain that the Lord protected me more times than I know, and I will never be able to thank Him enough.

One such example occurred in early 1973 when I was nearly gang-raped by a group of drug- and alcohol-influenced musicians. It was definitely a case of being at the wrong place at the wrong time. When one of them suggested to several others that they carry me into the bedroom, I headed for the door. I knew it was time to leave but one of the guys grabbed me. Terrified, I let out a blood-curdling scream, and––*thank God*––another one of the guys said, "Just let her go." Once the guy let go of my arm, I ran out of the apartment and took the long way back to my place.

After I was back at my apartment for about fifteen minutes, one of those guys showed up and started banging on the front door. Since I had no back door, I would have had to climb out the bedroom window to escape. I was so frightened when I returned home that I had got a pan of boiling water ready in case any of them came to harass me. I was planning to throw the water on this guy if he broke into my apartment. I *thank God* that after talking to the young man for a few minutes he told me he had come to apologize. He left quickly after doing so, and I never had anything to do with that group of people again.

I am still amazed at the love God has shown me even though I was living so foolishly in many areas of my life.

After coming to my senses, I asked my parents if I could move back into their house in the summer of 1973. I started getting my life on the right path again by registering at a technical-vocational school. Shortly thereafter, I was attending school full time and working part time. I was also helping my parents financially when my father was out of work because of heart problems. Then I met another "wonderful" man and quickly fell head over heels in love with him.

I only saw Sam (not his real name) on the weekends since he lived in another state. Our relationship consisted of talking on the phone during the week and spending every weekend together. Sam brought me flowers, and he took me out to dinner and dancing every time we were together. I was overwhelmed by this whirlwind romance. I thought he was my "Prince Charming."

In December 1974, I graduated with a certificate in Electronics Technology. Then I made, what I now know was another very unwise decision, and married Sam just a few days after graduation. I had been in this relationship with him for less than six months.

After we got married, I moved with Sam to a Native American reservation, where he was a teacher. Although he was working on the reservation, Sam was not a Native American. The reservation was an extremely isolated place and I could not get a job there because you had to be Native American or related to one in order to work in a privately-owned business. So, I began a repair service for electronic equipment at home. It kept me busy and helped us a little financially.

Of course, as most newly married wives do, I thought that we would live "happily ever after." To my complete shock and utter amazement, less than a week after we got married, I found out that Sam was incredibly physically and emotionally abusive.

He began hitting me only days after our wedding and, on several occasions, he even picked me up and threw me. I never knew what would set him off. One day, when he was out of control and in a rage, he bent over at the waist, ran towards me, and knocked me down. Another time, when I was crying after he had thrown me, Sam shook his fist at me and said, "If you don't shut up, I will beat the daylights out of you!" I knew that he meant it and I got quiet immediately. Sam always apologized afterwards, but the abuse increased and eventually it occurred almost on a daily basis.

Since I was raised to believe that once you got married, you stayed married no matter what, I did not tell anyone about the abuse. I was afraid of Sam and he knew it. *I felt trapped.* The physical isolation of living in the middle of nowhere, along with believing marriage was forever, was an awful combination. I would have stayed in that marriage and probably not be alive today if it were not for the Lord's mercy. I *thank God* for His mercy and intervention!

At the end of June 1975, we celebrated our six-month anniversary with flowers, dinner and gifts. Sam wrote me the most beautiful letter about how much he loved me and how he hoped the next six months would be as wonderful as the first six months had been for him. Two days later, Sam announced that he was divorcing me. He said that I was "not good for the marriage." I figured that meant I was not a good enough punching bag. I was doing everything I could to be a good wife. Now, my world was falling apart.

I was distraught and had suicidal thoughts after Sam moved out of the dorm room, where we were living while we were taking summer classes at a university. The emotional pain was indescribable! I called a crisis hotline for help. The sweet young lady on the other end of the phone had no idea what to say about my situation, but just being able to talk to someone helped a little. I thought I was going to lose my mind. Later I realized that the Lord permitted the divorce to deliver me out of a terrible situation even though I thought divorce was worse than the abuse at the time. God knows so much more than we can ever imagine!

During and after this extremely traumatic situation, the loving support of my parents was an invaluable part of my recovery. Of course they were furious at Sam when they found out about the abuse. However, they reached out to me unconditionally and helped me move back to New Mexico.

Shortly after returning to New Mexico, I was hired by a contract company to work at the Los Alamos Scientific Laboratory (LASL), which was subsequently renamed, the Los Alamos *National* Laboratory (LANL).

About a year later, I was hired to work directly for LASL. I also began taking night classes at the University of New Mexico in electrical engineering and laser technology. I had a really busy schedule but still made time to party, act crazy away from work and school, and live how I wanted to live. God was not on my mind, let alone in my heart. Unfortunately, I had not yet learned my lesson about making unwise choices.

Again, in spite of this, the Lord's hand was on me one hot summer day in 1976 when I was driving back to Los Alamos from Albuquerque. I had been working in a garden from six in the morning until noon and was very tired. My car had no air conditioning and I fell asleep at the wheel on a particularly dangerous part of the interstate highway. The car went off the road. When I woke up and saw a drainage ditch in front of me, I blacked out. After I regained consciousness, I realized that the car was sideways in the ditch, and I heard liquid running out of it. I quickly unbuckled my seat belt and got out of the car. A few minutes later, I found out it was only antifreeze coming out of the damaged radiator. *Thank God!*

Several people witnessed my car leaving the road and crossed the interstate to help me. One of them drove me back to Albuquerque to the police department, where my mother was working at the time. She took me to an emergency room to get checked out. *Miraculously,* I had only received minor sprains, cuts and bruises. Still, this did not cause me to turn my life around. I took so much for granted. I am extremely thankful that the Lord never gave up on me!

In 1980, after being involved for almost five years with men who were not willing to make a commitment, I met my current husband, Bob, at work. Since my first date at eighteen years old, my experiences with men had not gone well—to say the least—and after the divorce, I was determined to never get into a serious relationship with anyone again. I was *deeply* wounded. Shortly after I met Bob, I told him that if he ever hurt me physically I would kill him. *I meant it.* Amazingly, that did not scare him away, and he continued to pursue a relationship with me. We continued seeing each other in spite of my hardened heart. I was still trying to stay safe and dated other guys for a while so as not to get too close to Bob.

The Lord had another plan. Bob and I fell in love and our other relationships were ended a few months later. We got married on July 24, 1981. All was not a bowl of cherries though. Bob brought a lot of baggage from past trauma into our relationship as well. He had been married before and went through an emotionally shattering divorce. *What a pair.* It is a miracle we stayed together long enough to get married. We partied hard trying to numb the pain, but all that did was cause more problems. We became very good at hurting and blaming each other.

A month after we got married, Bob's answer to dealing with things was to accept a job that required him to work at an out-of-state location for LASL from Mondays through Fridays. I cried on the way home each time I took him to the airport. My heart was being broken *on a continual basis.* He was gone almost every week and when he returned home, he was so exhausted that we had no life together. He came home. He slept. I did the laundry. He left again.

Bob had assured me before transferring to this position that the traveling would decrease significantly the second and subsequent years but it did not. The painful cycle went on for four years until I told him that I would leave him if he did not get a job with a different group, where he could be at home. He did transfer but his new job was not a good situation either. It required him to work rotating shifts. One week, he worked days. The next week, he worked swing shift, and he worked graveyard the following week. He was living at home but he was either not there or sleeping. Our marriage had suffered greatly during the four years we were apart, and this new job did not help at all. Things just continued to deteriorate between us.

To complicate things even further, we went through the deaths of both our fathers in a little over a year. I had two major and one minor surgery during that same period. In 1982, Bob's mother came to live with us for several months which helped our relationship a lot. Not! She and I did not get along well. Bob's parents did not approve of our marriage from the beginning, and they made that very clear. That stress only added to our marriage issues. We also went through the emotional pain of infertility, and the possibility of conceiving a baby ended in 1983 when I had a hysterectomy at only thirty years of age.

So, I asked Jesus Christ into this mess on October 16, 1986, and expected that everything would get better. That was an incorrect assumption. In most areas, things did not become instantly better between us, but we continued to function quite well in spite of the immense emotional pain we were each carrying. We were both hurting so much inside and did not know how to get free.

Bible reading, memorizing Scripture, attending church and Bible studies, and many other Christian activities were all part of our attempt to make our lives and relationship better. We started attending Christian marriage conferences and things improved to some extent. We kept trying to live the Christian life in our own strength.

Then, in 1988, we were blessed to adopt a baby girl. Bob and I were ecstatic! The name we selected means *God's gracious gift*. Having a baby to care for added another dimension to the blessings and challenges in our already emotionally complicated lives. Regardless of the challenges, the adoption of our daughter was an answer to prayer. We saw the Lord move in supernatural and miraculous ways on our behalf which even amazed the people at the adoption agency. Over the years, we learned a lot about raising an adopted child and the unique spiritual implications involved in that process. Through it all, God has been so faithful.

Five years later, in spite of relying on the Lord to help me get through each day and all our efforts to stay together with the immense load of emotional baggage we carried, things were at the breaking point. After sticking it out for twelve years, I was seriously ready to leave Bob. Pain and trauma from the past had built up to the point that I could no longer ignore it. Things Bob did caused emotional pain from the past to come to the surface. It was overwhelming at times, and I could not handle it. My reactions were not pretty. What Bob was doing may not have been good, but my reactions were often way out of proportion to the circumstances. The same thing was happening to Bob. I was unintentionally causing pain from his past to come to the surface as well. It was an endless cycle.

Over the past several years we have learned that out of proportion reactions, or completely inappropriate reactions to situations, are often signs of past pain and trauma that has been buried. It may have been buried but it is very much alive and can erupt at any time like a volcano. Trauma includes physical abuse, spiritual abuse, emotional abuse, mental abuse, verbal abuse, molestation, rape, death of a loved one, divorce, accidents and natural disasters.

We had both experienced a great deal of pain and trauma before we met, and then we added to the already heavy load in our own relationship. We did not understand what was happening in our hearts. I *thank God* that He supernaturally intervened to get us on

His path of healing and freedom! We have now experienced huge amounts of freedom from past pain and trauma through Jesus Christ. As Jesus released much of the emotional pain, the eruptions occurred less often and became less intense. *Praise God!*

However, in 1993, my solution to the intense pain was to run away from Bob, the one who, I thought, was the cause of the pain. This would not have been good on so many levels. The praise and testimony about this is that the Lord orchestrated circumstances for our inner healing to finally begin. Some close friends of ours had just learned about and been trained in a ministry for Christian married couples called *Marriage Ministries*. They had prayed for the Lord to send them some couples in need. We were part of the answer to their prayers.

I will never forget the trip to the orientation in Santa Fe in their motorhome. We were so upset that they kept us separated. Bob sat in one part of the RV and I sat in the opposite end. The meeting we attended was an introduction to the ministry, and at the end, the women prayed with me and the men prayed with Bob. All I could do was cry. That was the start of the healing of our marriage.

We attended the thirteen-week *Marriage Ministries* class, and by our graduation, we were doing much better. We were asked to co-lead the next class and then the one following that. Were we completely free? No, but we were more free than at any time in the past. *Praise the Lord!* Our freedom and healing increased with each class, and it is still in process today.

The healing journey is just that—a journey. We receive freedom in layers and the Lord knows how much any one person can handle at a specific time in their life. It is like peeling an onion, one layer at a time. Jesus is not in a hurry, and He uses those who are a work in progress or He would have no one to serve Him. We are all a work in progress! The disciples were a good example of this. Why should Christians today be any different? Expecting perfection from those who follow Jesus Christ is not realistic and dumps guilt and condemnation on people.

The enemy of our souls, Satan, is a master of making people feel that because they are not perfect, they are either not saved or not good enough to serve God. If Satan can convince Christians of this, he can tremendously hinder God's work on this earth. We had to be set free from this lie.

This does not mean that we are given a blank check to intentionally sin and behave in ungodly ways. We are all accountable to God for what He shows us, and He expects us to repent for our known sin. Repentance, or changing the way we think to line up with God's thoughts about sin, helps us to be changed into His image. *We must be serious about repentance.* Only *godly sorrow* produces repentance. As our thoughts line up with God's about our behavior, the change in our actions will follow. It is a process.

Many people accuse Christians of being hypocrites if they are not living sinless, perfect lives. Show me a person who claims to be sinless and perfect and I will show you someone who is deceived or willingly untruthful. Christians who have been walking with the Lord longer usually admit they have not "arrived." The more we come to know God, the more clearly we can see our own imperfection. God does not require perfection from us. He only asks us to love Him with all our heart as Jesus said in Matthew 22.

> *Jesus said to him, "You shall love the LORD your God with **all your heart**, with all your soul, and with all your mind."*
> (Matthew 22:37, emphasis added)

As we seek to love God with all our heart, all our soul, and all our mind, He will enable us to become more like Him. Pain and trauma from the past can significantly hinder our ability to love God. Much of our sin is a direct result of the pain we are carrying from the past.

It can be a vicious cycle. To repent and remain free from that sin, we must be set free from the pain and trauma we have stuffed for years. It is not an easy process but it is worth it.

God loves us beyond anything we can imagine! He knows our hearts better than we do. He forgives us when we ask Him based on the *finished* work of His Son, Jesus Christ. We can do nothing to improve that sacrifice nor can we do anything to make ourselves instantly perfect. Our perfecting is a process that is accomplished over our lifetime, not all at once. God's mercy and grace allow for the process to happen—when we obey God—as He reveals places in us that need His healing touch and how to receive freedom.

The problem has been that many Christians know they are in need of healing, but they do not know how to receive it. Many things help the healing process such as those mentioned above, and I will discuss several others in the following chapters. Healing hearts is why Jesus Christ came, died, and rose again!

> *The Spirit of the Lord GOD is upon Me, because the LORD has anointed Me to preach good tidings to the poor;* **He has sent Me to heal the brokenhearted,** *to proclaim liberty to the captives, and the opening of the prison to those who are bound;*
>
> (Isaiah 61:1, emphasis added)

Total healing and freedom comes the day
we leave this world and enter heaven.

Chapter Two

The Early Years of Ministry

But as for me and my house, we will serve the LORD.

—Joshua 24:15

After Jesus became my best Friend, I started serving Him right away. I first volunteered as treasurer for Faith Baptist Church, Pastor Rick and Janet's church, which we were attending. I was so grateful for what the Lord had done in my life, and I wanted to help in any way possible. I did not try to begin serving God in a key position nor did I do what I did with the intention of "moving up." My heart was to just serve the Lord. I also did not wait to serve the Lord until I was completely free and healed. Total healing and freedom comes the day we leave this world and enter heaven. *Praise God!*

When Faith Baptist Church closed after Pastor Rick and Janet moved to California, I continued to find ways to serve at the next several churches we attended. Whether it was taking care of the cleaning supplies or cleaning, I did whatever was needed. In the meantime, I prayed.

The Lord developed my prayer life over the years, and I began praying for and with people, seeing the hand of God heal and deliver them from all kinds of problems. As I continued to witness miraculous answers to prayer, I desired even more to bring the needs of God's children before His throne.

However, in 1990, I developed a health problem diagnosed as biliary dyskinesia. This was an excruciatingly painful condition in which the bile duct from the liver to the intestines does not open properly to allow the bile to flow. This causes the duct to expand like a balloon. The pain is similar to a gallbladder attack when a person has gallstones. I know because I had those in the past and had my gallbladder surgically removed prior to this illness.

The doctors tried every possible treatment, including experimental surgical procedures, to give me relief from the horrible attacks of pain, but to no avail. After over a year of medical treatment, a doctor finally told me that I would have to live with this condition the rest of my life and take Demerol, a very potent, narcotic pain killer. He told me that he had consulted with a specialist at the Mayo Clinic who was willing to see me, but that doctor had no hope he could do anything else to help me. I was only thirty-seven years old and not willing to accept this prognosis of having to live with excruciating pain and rely on narcotics!

Then, a friend told me about a healing crusade to be held in Phoenix, and we went there praying for a miracle for our two-year-old daughter who had been diagnosed with asthma several months earlier. If I was healed that would be great, but I was really praying that the Lord would heal our precious little girl. It is an awful thing to watch your child suffer with an illness, and a horribly helpless feeling when they are struggling to breathe.

At the crusade, our daughter got hot all over. She was completely healed and set free from the asthma! I was so grateful to God for healing her. When we returned home, I took our daughter to the pediatrician and told the doctor that she had no asthma symptoms and no longer needed the medication. The doctor agreed that something miraculous had occurred. *Praise the Lord!*

As for me, I felt heat in my abdomen during the first service at the crusade, and I believed that God had miraculously healed me. I tested it by eating foods that would have certainly caused an attack in the past year, and there was no pain. *Praise the Lord!* The relief from that excruciatingly painful condition was complete and remarkable. I was so extremely thankful to the Lord for healing our daughter and me that I told Him I would do anything—serve Him in any way. He took me up on my offer, and shortly after returning from Phoenix, the Lord impressed on my heart that He wanted us to remodel our garage and open a Christian bookstore!

When I told Bob what I felt the Lord wanted us to do, he was very surprised at first. Bob prayed and eventually agreed to do it. It was exceedingly important that we were in unity about it because opposition from the devil started immediately. I will be sharing further about spiritual warfare and the adversity the enemy brings our way when we become sold-out for the Lord in a later chapter. For now, suffice it to say that we became huge targets for the kingdom of darkness.

As we proceeded to prepare to obey the Lord in this endeavor, we saw miracle after miracle happen. I had asked for used carpeting to be installed in the bookstore because I did not want the exposure to the chemicals in new carpeting. We had been told by the contractor that we would *never* find used carpeting available that time of year. It was March. The very next day, as I was in the downtown area of Los Alamos, I spotted rolls of used carpeting outside a department store! I hurried home and Bob returned with me to purchase what we needed for the bookstore. The contractor was shocked. I knew that God would supply.

> *And my God shall supply all your need according to*
> *His riches in glory by Christ Jesus.*
>
> (Philippians 4:19)

All our needs had been supplied by the Lord from the time that I asked Him into my life. This was no different. The Lord also arranged for the building permit to be approved in record time and for the building inspector, the man who signed the permit, to be at our house on the day the Bible display case was delivered. He asked if he could see our permit and was surprised to learn that he had signed it. Then, he helped Bob move the display case into the bookstore. *God is so good!*

The bookstore, *Rainbows and Sonshine*, opened on May 1, 1991. We were able to get the construction completed, order all the fixtures, order merchandise, and prepare for the opening in *less than sixty days* in spite of difficulties we encountered along the way. That was another miracle! The Lord provided over and over. He knew the store was always a ministry outreach and not a business endeavor. Our faithful God knows our hearts and honored our requests for supernatural intervention during the whole process.

In a very short time, the bookstore became a center for prayer ministry. About a month after opening *Rainbows and Sonshine*, a young mother came into the store with her twin baby girls in a double stroller. I could sense that she was brokenhearted as she told me the twins had been diagnosed with Hydrocephalus. It is a buildup of fluid inside the skull that leads to brain swelling. *Hydrocephalus* means "water on the brain." These precious babies' heads were significantly larger than normal and growing quickly. Their mother told me that the doctors said that they would need surgery to implant shunts to drain their heads. I assured her that I would pray and ask God to heal them.

As I was praying a few days later, I felt that the Lord wanted me to tell this young mother that her babies would be healed and not need the surgery. It was a huge step of faith for me to think about calling this lady I barely knew and tell her what I believed that the Lord had said. I did it, and although she seemed glad to hear from me, I could tell that she was still seriously concerned for her babies. Not long after that—*Praise God*—the babies were miraculously healed and did not need the surgery!

The girls' mother shared with me, years later, that my words helped get her through the doctors' visits when everything pointed to the surgery still being their only hope. She said that her faith was strengthened by mine. I am so grateful that I was obedient and called her when the Lord prompted me to do so. My faith was not always at that same level though. The Lord has given me increased levels of faith at different times, and He still does. He knows what we need and when we need it to accomplish His purposes!

A few months after opening the bookstore, I received a packet of advertising postcards in the mail. One of them was from the *Christian Booksellers Association* (CBA). They were going to have a drawing for two free scholarships to their upcoming weeklong booksellers' school in Colorado Springs. Our store was very small, only 169 square feet, and we were not eligible to join the CBA because the store was not located in a retail space. Why would the Lord want me to attend the school? I was just getting started with the store and had my hands full already. I tossed the card into the trash. The Lord told me to get it out and send it in. However, when I looked at the date of the drawing, I discarded it again. I did not *think* there would be enough time for them to receive the card from New Mexico before the drawing. Again, the Lord told me to get it out and send it in. He was persistent, and I am extremely grateful that He did not give up. I retrieved the card, filled it out, and mailed it that day.

Less than two weeks later, I received a registered letter in the mail from the CBA. I had won one of the scholarships! I attended the school with a thankful heart even though I could not imagine how the things I learned could be helpful for our tiny store. Obviously, my vision for the store was not large enough. Our little minds cannot comprehend God's magnificent ways but as we learn to trust and obey Him, our lives become increasingly exciting! The information shared at the school became enormously valuable in managing the store for the Lord in the future.

As the customers came and the demand grew, it became obvious in December 1992 that we needed a larger space for the store. Bob checked the rent prices for retail space in town. However, due to the Los Alamos National Laboratory's use of much of it for offices, the prices were outrageously high. I had no idea how we could possibly move the bookstore into any of the empty locations. So, I did what I always did when I had no idea how something would work out. I prayed. God knew how it would come to pass.

The Lord answered those prayers by sending a Christian man, Mark (not his real name), to see me in mid-January 1993. He owned a large retail business in town. Mark was getting ready to expand his store into a store space next to his and offered us all or any part of it for us to relocate the bookstore. He would be our landlord and set our rent at a remarkably reasonable amount that we could afford. We did not know Mark and had never met him before. The Lord had put it on Mark's heart to help us have a larger space for the bookstore after his wife visited the store. We accepted Mark's amazing offer. He paid for the wall to be constructed separating the stores and for the carpeting and its installation. Of course, the spiritual warfare increased again, but God continued to move in miraculous ways on our behalf.

We all found out a few days later, when the snowpack started melting, that there were major problems with leaks of the new location's roof. In fact, the whole area—over 2,400 square feet—needed a new roof. The lease that Mark had already signed with the shopping center's owner stipulated that Mark would be responsible for any repairs. Mark did not have the money to replace the roof. So, we prayed. I told Bob that this was no problem for God. Noah had more water than this to deal with and the Lord took care of him. The Lord had given me a high level of faith once again. Bob and Mark did not have the same level of faith I had at that point because they saw the water running down the walls and puddles of water all over inside the building. It seemed to be an "impossible" situation. Nevertheless, *all things are possible with God.* God was faithful and answered our prayers! Astoundingly, the shopping center owner agreed to pay for a new roof only a few days after refusing to do so. This was an incredible blessing for us and Mark. *Praise the Lord!*

The next "problem," or opportunity for the Lord to intervene, was that the weather in Los Alamos in February was not conducive to replacing a roof. It needed to be at least sixty degrees for that to happen. The snow—over two feet of it on the roof—had only just begun to melt. We were supposed to move in on March 1. It could have literally been months for the temperature to rise and stay as high as required for the work to be done on the roof. So, we prayed and God answered again! Within days, it warmed up for a week to over sixty degrees *every day* causing the local ice rink to close very early in the season. The building got its new roof, and we moved into the new location on March 1, 1993.

During the following five and a half years, the Lord provided for us and the store in incredible ways dozens and dozens of times. The prayer ministry grew rapidly as both men and women from many different churches and denominations came into the store and asked for prayer. Some of their prayer needs were *very* personal and serious.

We had a couch in the back room where I would take the ladies to pray with them if they desired prayer right away. I prayed with the men out front and was astonished at how transparent some of them were when they shared their situations with me. They felt safe because we were not connected to their church, and we always kept everything that they told us confidential. The Lord continued sending us people in need of healing in their bodies, hearts, minds, and spirits. His compassion and love for hurting people also became stronger in me.

I realized that many Christians and non-Christians alike were deeply wounded and searching for freedom from their emotional pain. One day, a young woman came into the store and headed straight for the cult/occult section of the books. I went over to ask if I could help her find anything. She seemed unusually nervous and answered, "No, thank you." I looked down at her arms, and they were covered in what appeared to be cigarette burns. Only seconds later, a man came in, walked up to her, and asked her what she was doing in *this* store. He was obviously angry. They immediately left. My heart was heavy for her. I prayed for her many times after that encounter but, as far as I know, she did not return to the store. The need for healing and freedom from pain and trauma is endless!

I had the opportunity to pray with several parents who came into the bookstore requesting information about the occult, especially about Wicca, from a Christian perspective. Many of the teens were being lured into occult practices in Los Alamos. Wicca 101 was even offered as a class and being presented at the public library. Therefore, we began carrying books and videos on those subjects to help get the information out to those in need of it.

One couple came into the bookstore on a Saturday afternoon, and they were visibly shaken up. They had been hiking in the mountains near Los Alamos with their three young daughters and their dog. While on their hike, they encountered a man dressed in a black robe. He began chanting and casting spells on them. Of course, they ran out of the area as fast as they could and drove directly to the bookstore. They were frantic when they asked, "What kind of place is Los Alamos?" The family had recently moved to town.

What a horrible trauma for them and their children to experience. I prayed with them, explained the reality of the number of people practicing the occult in the area, and suggested a few books to help them get educated. The couple was extremely grateful, and I was blessed to be able to help them.

Another mom was desperate for prayer one day when she came to the bookstore after her twelve-year-old daughter spent the night with a friend. Sobbing deeply, this mother told me that her daughter had been invited to a sleepover at her friend's house but she was opposed to it. However, her husband was more open-minded and felt that their daughter should be allowed to go. She gave in against her better judgment. Once at the house, their daughter was introduced by her friend's parents to the pentagram drawn on the living room floor. They were practicing Wiccans (witches). According to this mom, the girlfriend's parents explained the Wiccan ceremonies to this unsuspecting preteen. They showed her the ceremonial stick with raven feathers on it and asked her if she wanted to join them later. She said, "No," and the two girls left the house to go for a walk.

Sometime later, the girls returned for dinner. The visiting girl had spent the whole night at that house but the next day, she had no memory of anything that happened after dinner! Her mom had come to the bookstore asking for prayer and for someone to pray with her distraught daughter who was at home. I prayed with the mom and connected her with a pastor and his wife who later ministered to the mom and daughter. This was such a heartbreaking situation, and it contributed to my growing compassion for those traumatized in similar ways.

When we opened *Rainbows and Sonshine* out of obedience to the Lord, I had no idea that we would be praying with people who were so deeply wounded and traumatized. The Lord taught me volumes as the years passed and, as He did, my desire soared to help people receive freedom in every area. All this experience did not come without a price though. As I prayed with and educated larger numbers of people who were being unwillingly exposed to Wicca and the occult, there was a marked increase in the adversity we faced from people practicing those things.

When we began selling the book, *Wicca, Satan's Little White Lie*, we came under intense pressure to stop selling it. We were even threatened with legal action by a Wiccan coven in the area if we continued to have that book on our shelves. We did not give in to the pressure but there was an enormous amount of spiritual warfare associated with the entire matter. I *praise the Lord* that He helped us along that path and gave us wisdom, guidance, and protection from those who wanted to silence us. *God is faithful.*

We also experienced pressure from other Christians to just be a "nice" Christian bookstore and not sell anything with information about any cults. They did not understand that we had to obey the Lord in spite of potentially painful and traumatic situations we might experience as a result. Even some pastors in town got involved in back and forth editorials in the local newspaper with others who were upset with us. Interestingly enough, the pastors were not always supportive of us in this area and several of them were of the opinion that we should just leave other people alone and mind our own business. As a result, the Lord taught me—on a new level—about the importance of forgiveness in my own journey of inner healing.

One day, after a rather upset customer did not get what she wanted and left speaking unkind things to me, the Lord told me that I must consciously and verbally forgive everyone that had said hurtful things about me or the bookstore right away. I forgave them right then and there, and continue to practice forgiveness as being in ministry gives a person much opportunity to do so. "Sticks and stones may break my bones but words will never hurt me" is absolutely ridiculous. Words can and often do inflict more pain than any physical harm a person can experience. Emotional pain can be debilitating. Forgiveness is essential in receiving freedom and healing from emotional pain and trauma.

However, I have since prayed with several Christians who had been so wounded by others, including other Christians, that they had not been able to forgive those people. Of course, they were suffering emotional pain from the situations. They also knew what God's Word says about forgiveness. They just could not reconcile the two. I have learned in the past several years that sometimes emotional healing has to take place before a person can forgive the one who caused the pain and trauma. It is not that they are being willfully disobedient to the Lord. The truth is that the emotional pain is so overwhelming it can sometimes block their ability to forgive.

The cognitive choice to say *I forgive* is often easier when one has *not* gone through severe abuse of some kind, including but not limited to emotional, physical, mental, sexual, spiritual or satanic ritual abuse. Many Christians would disagree with this but my experiences have proven otherwise. Once Jesus releases the pain and trauma from someone who has been emotionally wounded, forgiveness frequently flows spontaneously from their heart. That is a beautiful process to witness!

This leads me to another very important topic for discussion. That is the pervasive problem in the Body of Christ of hastily forming opinions about others, especially other Christians. I don't care how *normal* someone may look or act in public or how abnormal they may act, unless you know every part of their journey on this planet, be careful what you allow yourself to think and believe about them. I will discuss some specific examples of this in a later chapter.

Christians from all denominations and nondenominational churches came into *Rainbows and Sonshine*, many of whom would not enter a church because they had been so wounded by other Christians or church organizations. They did not need to be judged for their current churchgoing status or personal issues. They needed to be shown the love and compassion of Jesus to enable them to advance in their healing journey. They did not need a repeat of what they had already been subjected to—judgmental and condemning words. This is one of the things I learned during the seven and a half years of serving the Lord in the bookstore. It did not happen overnight but I gradually realized that people would share their intimate prayer requests with me because they felt safe in doing so. If we are going to follow in the footsteps of Jesus, we must also learn to walk in His compassion for those who are emotionally wounded.

But when He saw the multitudes, He was moved with compassion for them, because they were weary and scattered, like sheep having no shepherd.

(Matthew 9:36)

Another thing I began learning during this period of ministry was that although we should be "moved with compassion," that does not mean we are to allow people to deceive us or take advantage of us. Setting godly, healthy boundaries are so important if you are going to run the race and stay in it to the end. People will test your boundaries just like children test the boundaries with their parents. It is not a sin or an ungodly practice to protect yourself from exhaustion and unreasonable demands from others.

Saying no is something that the Lord began teaching me when I came close to burnout. The hours I spent at the bookstore varied from ten to sixteen per day, six days a week. Just the sheer number of hours was enough to cause exhaustion let alone the emotional drain that came along with it. I *praise God* that I listened when He spoke to me about setting boundaries. I would not be in ministry today had I not entered that part of the Lord's training academy. Of course, *saying no* applies only to people and *not* to the Lord. He will never ask us to do anything that He does not give us the strength and guidance to accomplish. God is so faithful. *Praise the Lord!* I will discuss some other ministry struggles, trials, and lessons learned in the next chapter.

My brethren, count it all joy when you fall into various trials, knowing that the testing of your faith produces patience.

(James 1:2-3)

Chapter Three

Trials, Trauma, and Lessons Learned

In the late spring of 1998, the Lord gave me a very unsettled feeling about continuing with the status quo. I know that feeling all too well. It is like something ready to explode inside of me and if I don't pay attention to it, I will miss what the Lord wants to reveal to me. This is never an easy or comfortable place to be, but it is His way of speaking to me. It usually happens before a time of transition or major change in my life. I will be addressing more about transitions later. Let me just stress the importance of *listening carefully* to the Lord during these times.

At first, Bob and I thought that we were going to sell the bookstore, and we pursued that path for a short time. There were three couples interested in purchasing the store but two of them were unable to secure the finances needed, and the sale to the third couple was discouraged for us by the Lord. So, it became clear that the Lord was asking us to close *Rainbows and Sonshine*. Close the bookstore? We really had to pray and pray *and pray* about that to be sure we were hearing the Lord correctly.

The bookstore was doing well financially and had been making a profit for several years. There were over three thousand customers on the mail list from all over northern New Mexico and Albuquerque. Employees of the Los Alamos National Laboratory would shop at the bookstore on their lunch hour or after work. How could we close it? It was a tremendously difficult decision and not lightly entered into.

We had opened the bookstore from nothing, and now the Lord was asking us to close it. It made no sense in the natural, and we struggled with the decision for several weeks. The Lord is *always gracious* when we struggle with His requests. He *never* forces anyone to obey. He will *never* override our free will. That I know. But we had to be sure that it was His will and not ours or something from the kingdom of darkness. There were many people in town that wanted *Rainbows and Sonshine* to close and were praying against us and the bookstore.

When Bob and I were finally sure this was God's will, not knowing why, we made preparations to close the store. I made one hundred phone calls to our most faithful customers and let them know that we were going to have a "Christmas in August" sale to close *Rainbows and Sonshine*. That was our only advertising. People lined up outside the store before we opened on the first day of the sale! It was only ten days from the beginning of the sale until the day we closed. Ninety percent of the inventory flew out the door, and all the fixtures were sold as well. *Praise God!* It was another miracle.

Most people were supportive and encouraging even though we had no idea why the Lord was directing us in this way. Only a few were upset or angry about the decision. We forgave them. They had a hard time understanding how we could blindly obey the Lord when it made no sense at all. A few months later, we found out that our landlord, Mark, was selling his store and moving to another state. He had been our landlord for over five years and had provided a safety net between us and the owners of the shopping center. He also took a lot of heat on our behalf, and we will be *forever grateful* to him for his unwavering support. If we had not been obedient to the Lord about closing the store, we would have been subjected to a major increase in rent and God only knows what else with the owners of the shopping center. They were not the biggest fans of *Rainbows and Sonshine*. In fact, they disliked the bookstore and our uncompromising stand on many issues, including not celebrating Halloween with the rest of the stores in the shopping center. Sometimes standing up for the convictions that the Lord has placed in your heart brings persecution and struggles in this country of "freedom." Jesus warned us of this in John 15:18 and in Matthew 5:11-12.

"If the world hates you, you know that it hated Me before it hated you."

(John 15:18)

"Blessed are you when they revile and persecute you, and say all kinds of evil against you falsely for My sake. Rejoice and be exceedingly glad, for great is your reward in heaven, for so they persecuted the prophets who were before you."

(Matthew 5:11-12)

"Rejoicing and being exceedingly glad" during times of persecution and adversity is not always easy. However, as you go through these times with the Lord by your side—trusting His perfect will is being accomplished—you develop a "thicker" skin. I had to be alert regarding my human tendency to pick up offenses, and I practiced forgiveness time and time again. This is a challenge that I believe we all face our entire lives. It has gotten easier for me the closer I have gotten to Jesus.

Another trial that brought me great freedom in the end was happening the whole time I served the Lord in the bookstore. Shortly after opening *Rainbows and Sonshine*, I started having extremely scary episodes of tachycardia. My heart was racing above two hundred beats per minute, causing dizziness when that occurred.

At first, it happened infrequently, and we prayed for God to heal whatever was causing the problem. As time passed, the episodes became more frequent and lasted longer. After six years of praying and battling the kingdom of darkness over this, I finally talked to an acquaintance of mine who was a nurse and a Christian. She also went to the same church that Bob and I attended at the time.

What she said to me was not helpful at all. In fact, it hurt me a lot. This woman, who I believed was a very godly woman, told me that the problem would go away *if my walk with God was right.* I took those words to heart because she was in the medical field and also knew Jesus Christ as her Lord and Savior. This was emotionally and spiritually painful for me, and I cried out to God daily for Him to show me what I was doing that was causing this increasing health problem. It was now waking me up from a sound sleep at night, and producing shortness of breath and pain down my arm. I also blacked out several times due to the high rate of my heartbeat. I had been placed under condemnation by the words of this well-meaning Christian woman and delayed seeking medical help for another year as a result. I was definitely not walking in wisdom regarding this situation.

> *Wisdom is the principal thing; therefore get wisdom.*
> *And in all your getting, get understanding.*
>
> (Proverbs 4:7)

Getting wisdom is something we do all our lives in the midst of struggles, and hopefully, we learn the lesson the first time. If not, the Lord will allow us to go around that mountain again. This was a huge lesson that I will never forget and one mountain that I have never revisited. *Praise the Lord!*

When I finally went to a doctor, who turned out to be a Christian man, he did a number of tests and diagnosed that I had PSVT, a condition in which the heart develops an extra electrical circuit that causes the heart to race wildly. He did not make me feel foolish when he asked me why I waited so long to seek medical help. I told him that Bob and I had been praying and believing that God would heal me. That loving doctor said, "Yes, He can do that, but God uses doctors too."

After several trials of medications that did not help, the next step was a delicate heart procedure to turn off the extra electrical circuit. A specialist performed that surgery in November 1998. One of my prayers was that the specialist would also be a Christian. When I met him the evening before the surgery, He was wearing a cross around his neck. He also got down on his knees and prayed with a woman in the waiting room just before going in to perform the procedure on me. Bob witnessed the answer to our prayers right there in the waiting room. The surgery was successful the first time around, and other than a long recovery period of more than nine months, there were no complications from the procedure. *Praise the Lord!*

During my recovery, we were praying and seeking the Lord's will regarding His next ministry assignment for us. We continued to serve Him in the church we attended but we also felt that He had a plan for some other full-time ministry. In the meantime, the Lord had another major lesson to teach us regarding *the uncertainty of tomorrow and the importance of being flexible.*

It was May 4, 2000, and Bob and I were getting ready to take an overnight trip to Albuquerque to celebrate his birthday, which was the next day. However, a plume of smoke was rising from the nearby mountains. Since we would be leaving our daughter at home with a sixteen-year-old babysitter, we called the police to check on the fire. We were told that there was a controlled burn going on and that there was no danger to Los Alamos. We left for Albuquerque giving the babysitter instructions to take our daughter to her house in Espanola if she became concerned for their safety.

On our return trip home the next afternoon, we could not help but notice that the plume of smoke was *much* larger. Again, we called the police and were told the same thing as before. Something was not right. My spirit was really uneasy and I did not feel that we were being told the whole truth. The following day, the plume of smoke had grown significantly, and the smoke was coming right over our neighborhood. Our house was full of smoke, and I was having difficulty breathing. We talked at dinner about what we would do if we needed to leave town.

A few minutes after dinner, I called the police once again and was referred to a toll-free number that had been set up for questions regarding the fire. When I called, I was told that the fire had originally been started as a controlled burn but that it had gotten out of control. They were not expecting it to reach Los Alamos and had not ordered even a voluntary evacuation. Nevertheless, after speaking to that person, we made the decision to pack up our two vehicles and drive to Santa Fe.

Fifteen minutes after we left home, an evacuation was ordered for three areas in Los Alamos, including our neighborhood. We found a hotel in Santa Fe that would allow our poodle to stay in the room, and we watched the news for updates on the fire. For the next two days, we observed the smoke plume grow and were concerned for the people that were still in Los Alamos. According to the news reports, the authorities in Los Alamos were about to lift the evacuation order but the Lord told us otherwise. He was right. Less than thirty minutes later, the entire town of Los Alamos was ordered to evacuate.

It was chaos. Thousands of people were all trying to get out of town at once and the traffic jam was awful. Some of our friends reported that they were stopped on one of the bridges in town, and the traffic was bumper to bumper as they watched the flames coming down the canyon towards the bridge. It was terrifying for those people but *thank God*, everyone made it out of town who wanted to leave before the fire began devouring homes. The officials did not expect anything in Los Alamos to be left standing once the fire entered town. In the end, over four hundred families were left homeless and over 47,000 acres burned as a result of the Cerro Grande fire. Of course, our family and thousands of others had been praying for the Lord to intervene. God's mercy was all that prevented the firefighters' worst fears from coming to pass.

We were not among those whose homes were destroyed but many of our friends lost everything. The emotional pain and trauma that people suffered during this horrific event still affects many of their lives today. Our home was severely smoke-damaged and had to be professionally cleaned before we were able to move back into it a month after we left town. The trauma of seeing, on television, the fire burning homes—including many homes that belonged to friends and acquaintances—was enormous. I was heartbroken and shed many tears. I watched in unbelief as firefighters were hosing down our neighbor's house across the street from ours. Their house was spared from being one of those destroyed as a result. *Praise the Lord!*

The Lord has done an incredible amount of healing in my heart and mind regarding this trauma. As I write about it, I am sad that it happened and for those who lost all they owned, but I no longer feel the emotional pain that I once suffered. The Lord also taught me valuable lessons that I could not have learned without going through this experience.

First and foremost, the Lord *forever* solidified in my heart how temporary everything is in this life. What we know as *normal* life can be gone in a split second. We must always keep our eyes on Him no matter what the circumstances of life may bring our way. These verses in James 4:13-14 became reality for me.

Come now, you who say, "Today or tomorrow we will go to such and such a city, spend a year there, buy and sell, and make a profit"; whereas you do not know what will happen tomorrow. For what is your life? It is even a vapor that appears for a little time and then vanishes away.

I had all *my* plans for the week of May 7, 2000, and every one of them changed *in an instant.* This traumatic experience helped me learn to be increasingly flexible and less rigid in many ways. I have always been an organized type of person and did well when things went smoothly and according to plan. However, I used to struggle somewhat when unforeseen situations arose that changed the course of those plans or completely rearranged them. Those of you who are organizers can understand this. The fact is the Lord knows the beginning from the end and His plan is always the best plan. We have to seek to stay in alignment with Him. We have to be flexible to do this because He only gives us *part* of the plan at a time. Sometimes the part He gives us is a very small part. We fool ourselves into thinking that it is bigger and more far-reaching than He means it to be. So, we need to be consistent in saying the following.

"If the Lord wills, we shall live and do this or that."

(James 4:15)

"not My will, but Yours, be done."

(Luke 22:42)

In addition to the Lord teaching me many valuable lessons through the trauma of the Cerro Grande fire, my desire to serve Him became even stronger. I prayed extra diligently to know His will regarding our next assignment in ministry. I heard Him clearly. It involved another *major* change in our lives and in our plans.

Our plan was to pay off the mortgage on our house in the coming two years, retire, and travel around in an RV ministering to whomever the Lord put in our path. His plan was completely different from ours.

It involved applying with an international missions' organization and moving to Texas! Some friends of ours were on staff with the organization, and Bob asked me to call them to request applications. This was another trial and test of faith for me because I do not enjoy hot climates and the main office was in the Dallas Metroplex, a hot, humid, and tornado-prone part of Texas. Bob had lived in Los Alamos for forty-six years and I had lived there twenty-six years. This move to Texas would certainly be a drastic change if we were asked to join the staff.

After sending in our applications, we were invited to go to Texas for a weeklong interview. At the end of that week, they asked us to come and be part of the administrative team. We would first have to return home and raise support since none of those on staff were paid by the ministry. Raising support was a new undertaking for us but it went well, and in less than six months, we had the monthly support they suggested for our size family. Selling our home was the next hurdle that we had to clear.

The housing market in Los Alamos was in a slump at the time because so many homes were put up for sale after the Cerro Grande fire. It was overwhelmingly a buyer's market, and the real estate agent with whom we signed a contract was not hopeful that our home would sell very quickly. Nevertheless, we knew that God had gotten us this far in the process and that He would take care of this detail as well.

> *But Jesus looked at them and said to them, "With men this is impossible, but with God all things are possible."*
>
> (Matthew 19:26)

From man's perspective, we were in for a long wait to sell our home. It was January and there was three feet of snow on the ground. The real estate market was in an extremely depressed state.

Everything looked discouraging. But God had a plan. The sign went into the front lawn on Thursday night with only the top visible due to the snow. By Friday afternoon, we had an appointment to show the house to potential buyers the following Monday! The couple signed a contract to purchase our home on Tuesday evening. *"With God all things are possible!"*

That was the easy part. Now, we had to find a house in Texas, pack up a house and two sheds full of stuff, and move to tornado country. Finding the house in Texas was a little challenging but, with the Lord's help, we found one the fourth day we were there. Not coincidentally, one of the most emotionally painful experiences of my life happened that same day.

My mother, sister, niece, and nephew had been living together in a mobile home near Los Lunas, New Mexico. While we were looking at our new home in Texas, *their home was burning to the ground!* I cannot describe the emotional pain I felt knowing that they lost everything in the fire. It was hard to believe that this had happened, knowing that our home survived a major wild fire only seven months earlier. I *praised God* repeatedly that they were not at home at the time of the fire. I knew that the Lord would replace the destroyed items that could be replaced. Their lives were protected and that was what mattered most.

We returned to New Mexico and immediately went to help comfort them and do whatever we could to assist with the insurance claim and other needs they now had. This was a time of high levels of stress and trauma for us as we were preparing to move in less than a month while trying to be there for them. Some people asked us if we were still planning to move to Texas under the circumstances. They assumed that we would not go since my family had gone through this horrible tragedy. Those people did not understand that my family encouraged us to go and did not want this situation to prevent us from serving the Lord in Texas.

This attack from the enemy only made me more determined to go through with the Lord's directions. So, after a very tearful good-bye with family and friends, we drove two trucks to Texas on March 1, 2001, and began a new chapter in our lives. As you can probably imagine, this was the most heart-wrenching transition in ministry that we had to make to that point. Transition is never easy but this one was a bear!

*When the Lord asks us
to step out of our comfort zone,
it can be frightening and intimidating.*

Chapter Four

Transitions... Out of the Comfort Zone

As I said at the end of the last chapter, transition is never easy. Most human beings do not like change. However, without it, we can become too comfortable and stagnant in our lives and walk with the Lord. When the Lord asks us to step out of our comfort zone, it can be frightening and intimidating. He has led us through transitions several times over the past twenty plus years of ministry, and although it has been exciting in many ways, it has often been extremely difficult.

When the Lord impressed on me to remodel our garage and open a Christian bookstore, He took me *miles* out of my comfort zone. My training and experience was in electronics, electrical engineering, laser technology, and environmental medicine. I had taken no business classes in high school or college and had no idea how to do what He was asking of me. That is how He gets all the glory for the success of the assignment.

This transition into bookstore owner was a real challenge for me. Like Moses, I said, "But Lord, how can I do this?" I did not even like to read. The Lord said, "I will lead you and show you each step of the way." Through a friend of mine, the Lord introduced me to a wonderful, godly woman, Deloris, who had been a partner in the prior Christian bookstore in Los Alamos. It had closed four years earlier. When I called Deloris and explained the Lord's directions to me, she was exceedingly helpful and supportive. Deloris shared a wealth of information, and she was our first part-time employee. Where did my help come from?

My help comes from the LORD, who made heaven and earth.

(Psalm 121:2)

Deloris gave me the names and phone numbers of several Christian book distributors and publishers, greeting card publishers, and jewelry distributors. Nevertheless, once again, when I received the Bible catalog in the mail, I went into another "How can I do this?" mode. Until then, I thought that the King James Version was the only version of the Bible. This catalog was the size of a large phone book. Bob was encouraging and said, "The Lord has helped you this far; He will help you decide what Bibles to order." He was right. The Lord showed me which versions and what quantities to order. Of course, when I was selected to receive the CBA Booksellers' School scholarship, the Lord gave me a huge boost on the learning curve. *He is so good!*

One of the things they did not teach at the CBA School was how to deal with spiritual warfare when you've opened a Christian bookstore in the middle of a neighborhood populated by Wiccans. I don't think there is a class for that. This was a learning curve that Bob and I were not aware existed. We had no idea that Los Alamos County was a favorite area for people practicing witchcraft and the occult. That idea was not even on our radar. The church we were attending at the time did not believe in, nor teach about, spiritual warfare. We did not even recognize that what we were experiencing *was* spiritual warfare. So, we were on our own, and we got spiritually "beat up" for a time. But the Lord sent help!

God is our refuge and strength, a very present help in trouble.

(Psalm 46:1)

Within a few months of opening *Rainbows and Sonshine*, the Lord sent a man, who I had never met before, to talk to me. This sounds familiar, doesn't it? This Spirit-filled Christian man was getting ready to teach a class on spiritual warfare at the Episcopal Church. After he explained about the thirteen-week class, I said, "Thank you, but I don't think we would be interested." This man knew the spiritual climate in town and was very wise. He said, "That's fine. Just call me when you find a cross burning on your lawn." Wow! *That got my attention.* Bob and I decided to sign up for the class. The class was definitely the Lord's provision for us and the beginning of our education about spiritual warfare. I will discuss more about that subject in another chapter. By the way, no one ever burned anything on our lawn, but a lot of other things came against us that we were better prepared to deal with as a result of taking the class. *Praise the Lord!*

The season of transition that included closing the bookstore, undergoing my heart procedure, living through the Cerro Grande fire, my family losing their home to a fire, and moving to Texas was by far the most challenging one of our lives. The only way that we were able to experience and survive all of that change and trauma in such a short time was *by the grace of God.*

The Lord got us through but our hearts were broken in so many ways during that time. The bookstore was like a baby to me. I had watched it grow from nothing. Then, I had to close it and walk away. The Lord often asks us to do things that are painful at the time but He knows the bigger picture. He knows what we need to allow to die in order for a beautiful new thing to be birthed.

Hindsight is 20/20! Looking back, I can clearly see that the Lord was preparing us all along for personal ministry to those who have experienced pain and trauma. He uses *everything* in our lives to help us in what He calls us to do—if we will allow Him to do so. I know this without a doubt. Even though we thought we were going to Texas to be part of the administrative staff with the international missions' organization which we did, the Lord had a larger plan in mind.

While we were there, from 2001 to 2005, the Lord sent people into our lives apart from the ministry who needed prayer and to be shown the love of Jesus. One such couple, Tom and Mary (not their real names), were in the midst of the pain of battling infertility. We met Tom immediately after moving to Texas. He was a window specialist and our new home needed thirteen windows replaced due to the extreme heat conditions in that area. The day Tom came to replace the windows, his assistant was unable to come with him. So, Bob helped Tom with the window removal and installation. Bob and Tom talked about many things that day, including why we moved to Texas, and Tom got to hear our testimony.

Although they were Christians, Tom and his wife had not been attending church for a while. They had been hurt at their previous church and had not yet found a new one. The Lord allowed us to minister to them in a way that we never imagined.

Tom and Mary took us out to dinner as a thank-you for Bob helping Tom with the windows. We got to know them a little better, and a short time later, we invited them to our home for dinner. That evening, they shared that they had been trying to have a baby but had been unsuccessful in conceiving one. We understood this pain. The doctors had suggested they try in vitro fertilization, an extremely costly and emotionally exhausting procedure. Tom and Mary had already tried it twice with no success. They were praying about trying one more time the following week, but they were so drained financially and emotionally that they both had tears in their eyes as they asked us to pray with them.

The doctors had told Tom and Mary that there was only a ten percent chance that the third procedure would be successful since the other two had failed and Mary was in her early forties. Something rose up in me that was definitely from the Lord when I heard this. I said, "It doesn't matter what the doctors think. If they said you only have a ten percent chance of success, then that means you can be part of the ten percent!" Bob and I prayed over them with such faith and righteous anger against what the enemy was doing to them that they were encouraged and left smiling. Their wounded hearts were bandaged and their faith was strengthened. The Lord had, once again, taken us *out of our comfort zone.*

A few months later, we got the wonderful news that Mary was pregnant! Mary carried the baby the entire nine months with no complications or problems at all. Then He blessed them with a healthy baby boy. *Praise the Lord!* This was a testimony of the Lord's healing power. We were grateful that we had obeyed the Lord and ministered what He had spoken to us even though it was a little uncomfortable.

Bob also had opportunities to minister to wounded Christians as he was performing his job of courier with the missions' organization. After they got to know him, he prayed with people at the post office and bank on a regular basis. One lady and her daughter who were Catholics accepted Jesus Christ as their *personal* Lord and Savior after the mom had a conversation with Bob at the teller's window. *Praise the Lord!*

Another brokenhearted woman was put in my path as a result of me being diagnosed with fibromyalgia in late 2001. Susan (not her real name) was a massage therapist, and I began seeing her for therapeutic massage. During the very first appointment, I felt like I had known her for years, and the Lord gave me a boldness and freedom to share my heart with her immediately. That day, Susan had broken up with her tremendously violent boyfriend who had threatened her life. She was in tears as she shared the account of what had happened earlier. After she finished the massage, I prayed with her and she said, "I believe you were sent to me by God." The Lord knows exactly what He is doing!

Susan had been raised Christian but had gone through many emotionally painful and traumatic situations which slowly caused her to distance from the Lord. She was also wounded by other Christians which did not help matters at all. Susan needed the love and compassion of Jesus. I was happy to be available for that. It was also a mutually healing relationship since she was so gifted in massage therapy and had special training for treating people with fibromyalgia. My relationship with Susan grew over the next three and a half years. During that time, the Lord allowed me to help her in many spiritual areas, and she started calling me, "Pastor Kathy." It was our private joke, but when I was ordained in 2007, Susan said, "See, I knew it all along!"

The Lord showed Susan His love and compassion through me. Along with His love and compassion, relationship is a major aspect in the healing journey. We all need to be in godly relationships in order for the process of our inner healing and growth in Him to be nurtured.

Relationship was enormously important as we continued to minister to other people in Texas. One family we met and prayed with was from India and another was from Pakistan. We were also blessed to pray with several families that had been on staff with the missions' organization but were no longer with it for one reason or another. Broken hearts abounded in fellow Christians, and the Lord kept showing us how to pray with each one according to their specific need. *Our true calling in ministry was becoming increasingly defined.*

The next season of ministry began for us in June 2005 when the Lord directed us to return to New Mexico. We were asked to be the U.S. office managers for *Lifeline Ministries,* an outreach in Mexico at that time. Former pastors of ours from Los Alamos, Dave and Dee, were getting ready to move to Guaymas, Mexico, and they needed someone to do all of the administrative tasks here in the states.

After prayerfully considering it, we gladly accepted their invitation. However, this transition was not without heartache and trauma either.

Three days after we arrived back in New Mexico, a doctor told my sister and me that our mom had terminal lung cancer. She was seventy-seven years old, and the doctor did not recommend any treatment other than hospice care since the cancer was so advanced. For the next six weeks, we watched as my mother's condition quickly deteriorated. On July 20, 2005, my mom went to be with the Lord. My mom was a passionate believer, and her faith never once waivered right up to the end. She was an inspiration to me, and I have the assurance that I will see her again in heaven.

Although her passing came much quicker than the doctor had predicted, I believe it was an answer to prayer. She did not suffer, and most of the things the doctors and nurses said would happen before she died did not occur. *Praise the Lord!* Nevertheless, her passing was hard in other ways because my mom was our last living parent. When she died, my realization of the temporary nature of life was increased, and my desire to serve the Lord also increased. My mom's passing also stirred up some unresolved pain and trauma from the past. Bob and I began seeking additional help for new levels of freedom.

We registered for *Freedom Walk*, a weeklong, deliverance ministry that was offered in our area. It was a different method of inner healing that helped remove another layer of unwanted filth from our hearts. Many Christians do not believe that deliverance from demonic spirits is necessary for Christians, but that does not line up with our biblical understanding, training, or experience. Christians can definitely be oppressed and tormented by demons and the kingdom of darkness, but the blood of Jesus has the power to set us free if we will apply it appropriately. "Can a Christian have a demon?" is a topic discussed in many books. Therefore, I will not explain that any further. Suffice it to say that we definitely believe the kingdom of darkness, the devil, demons, and evil spirits do exist and can have a huge negative effect on a Christian's life.

One result of going through the *Freedom Walk* ministry for me was that I received the strength to finally discontinue the seven medications I had been taking for four years to treat fibromyalgia and medication side effects. The Lord had already prepared me to do so before we left Texas but He told me to wait until the time was right. Seven months after my mother's passing, I slowly began discontinuing the medication one by one. Everything went well until the last medication.

I did not realize that medication, Fentanyl, was a highly addictive, extremely powerful painkiller. It was a patch that I wore twenty-four hours a day, seven days a week. I did not know when I removed the patch that Fentanyl is approximately *one hundred times more potent than morphine.* Ten hours after I removed it, I went into full-blown withdrawal. I had cold sweats, hot sweats, uncontrollable shaking, and every organ in my body felt like it was going to explode. I was in bad shape! I searched the Internet to check Fentanyl out. What I learned gave Bob and I much reason for concern. According to the information that we found, most people cannot get off Fentanyl. The withdrawal procedures used by doctors included using tranquilizers and other medicines under close supervision or putting the patient into a drug-induced withdrawal in the intensive care unit of a hospital. My husband and I prayed and asked the Lord for His wisdom and guidance. In the meantime, I applied another patch and the horrible withdrawal symptoms subsided.

Once again, the Lord answered our prayers by telling both Bob and I to call a friend from church who was a pharmacist. That man was a godsend. He told me how to back off the Fentanyl, and I followed his directions. His wife had been on Fentanyl years before for cancer, and he had to help her back off the medication at one time. *Our God is awesome!*

I want to make something exceedingly clear about this. Please do not try this yourself. I have an extensive medical background, and the Lord led me step by step. If you are using any type of medication, I strongly recommend that you only change your dosage with the direct supervision of your doctor.

As I reduced the amount of time that I wore the Fentanyl patch, the withdrawal symptoms were still there but to a lesser degree. It took me about four weeks to completely stop that medication but I *praise God* that He enabled me to do it in His strength. It was not easy. While I was in the worst of the withdrawal, I could *not* feel His presence but I knew that I knew that He was with me. It was a very difficult time for me as I am normally exceptionally sensitive to the Lord's presence. That is when faith took over and got me through the days and nights. The enemy attacked me during that time as well, telling me to remember the pain I had before I was taking the medication and how I could not walk without help. I told that ungodly voice that I knew God had healed me and to get away from me in Jesus' name. Once I had completely discontinued the Fentanyl, God proved the enemy to be a liar again. I was healed of the fibromyalgia symptoms! *Praise the Lord!*

Another interesting opportunity came our way the day after I first removed the Fentanyl patch. A couple of friends of ours from church invited us to go to a home Bible study being taught by the Director of the *Healing Rooms* in Albuquerque. In spite of the absolutely awful way I felt physically, we went with them. At the end of the teaching, several of those in attendance prayed for me. They did not know what was going on, only that I was extremely ill. They also invited us to go to the *Healing Rooms* a few days later. We did that as well. I was hungry for whatever the Lord wanted to minister to me.

That began our involvement with the *Healing Rooms'* ministry. Our family went through the training and graduated from the program in December 2006. Bob and I became Assistant Directors the following year. We prayed with people for physical, emotional, and spiritual healing on Fridays and Saturdays for the next two and a half years. It was wonderful to watch the Lord heal people's bodies, minds, and hearts through healing prayer!

We also continued to serve as the Directors of the U.S. office for *Lifeline Ministries* until February 2008. In addition to our administrative duties with *Lifeline Ministries*, we coordinated the *Lifeline Ministries'* Christmas Shoebox Project each year. Between Thanksgiving and Christmas, we drove the fourteen hours to Guaymas with hundreds of shoeboxes and stuffed animals for the children in orphanages and work camps. We also had the privilege of praying with children and adults in Mexico when the Lord gave us opportunities to do so. With heavy hearts, we resigned from *Lifeline Ministries* to focus on personal prayer ministry, which the Lord had revealed was His main calling on our lives. This was another heart-wrenching decision and transition. However, knowing that the Lord was directing us gave us the peace to walk into the next season.

As we continued to minister in the *Healing Rooms*, our desire to see Christians set free from past pain and trauma grew. We realized that a lot of the emotional pain and trauma was causing physical illness, and we asked the Lord to show us more about helping people receive His healing and freedom. God answered that prayer when He supernaturally led me to Gary and Kathi Oates' website.

In January 2008, I was looking for a new CD by an artist that I discovered also led worship for Gary and Kathi Oates at some of their conferences. I then checked out their website where I noticed that they took missions' teams to South America several times a year. Bob and I had, a few weeks earlier, been told by one of the pastors at church that we would be traveling for the Lord to other countries including South America. I thought, "South America?" As I repeatedly looked at South America on the world map on our kitchen table, the Holy Spirit kept drawing my eyes to the Amazon River. I "thought" that it was highly unlikely we would ever travel to the Amazon River. Upon further investigation into the missions' trip that Gary and Kathi had scheduled for that November, I learned that it was to Manaus, Brazil, on the Amazon River! I was stunned. So, I talked to Bob about what I believed the Holy Spirit was showing me. After much prayer, Bob and I submitted our applications to go with Gary and Kathi to Manaus, Brazil, and we were accepted to be part of the team.

Since we would be going to the Amazon River with this couple, I decided to check out their website further and noticed that Kathi Oates had a strong calling to minister to the brokenhearted. I ordered a set of DVDs to learn what Kathi's approach was to healing the brokenhearted. Bob and I watched those DVDs but did not see how it would fit into the inner healing ministry we were already doing at the *Healing Rooms* and elsewhere.

Another surprising turn of events happened shortly after we watched those DVDs. A poster was put up at the church we were attending announcing the speakers for a conference that August. To our amazement, we saw that Gary and Kathi Oates were among the speakers scheduled to be part of that conference! We had no idea anyone at the church had invited them to come or even knew about their ministry. No one at the church knew that we were about to go with them to Brazil. When we told the assistant pastor, she asked if we would like to host Gary and Kathi while they were in Albuquerque. Of course, we said, "Yes." We had the wonderful privilege of spending four days getting better acquainted with them.

During Kathi's presentation at the conference, she mentioned a *Healing the Brokenhearted Ministry* training seminar that was going to be held in North Carolina in ten days. I had no intention of attending that seminar until two days later when the Lord told me to go. That morning, I asked Bob to pray about it, and he said that he did not need to pray because the Lord had already told him that I should attend the seminar. What a confirmation! So, I flew to North Carolina eight days later. My attendance at that seminar launched the *Healing the Brokenhearted Ministry* method of inner healing in New Mexico.

Since September 2008, Bob and I have been applying the *Healing the Brokenhearted Ministry* (HBH) process as we have prayed with several hundred Christian men, women, and children. It has been a tremendously rewarding season in our lives. This season also brought with it another transition when the Lord instructed us to resign from the *Healing Rooms* in May 2009 to focus completely on the *Healing the Brokenhearted Ministry*. We still use all the tools that the Lord has allowed us to learn over the years as we pray with people, and I am very grateful for the wealth of training and experience He has provided to us.

> *Teach me Your way, O LORD; I will walk in Your truth; Unite my heart to fear Your name.*
>
> (Psalm 86:11)

> *Teach me good judgment and knowledge, for I believe Your commandments.*
>
> (Psalm 119:66)

> *Teach me to do Your will, for You are my God; Your Spirit is good. Lead me in the land of uprightness.*
>
> (Psalm 143:10)

We must be willing to let Him teach us, take us through transitions, and lead us into new seasons. Sometimes, betrayal, discussed in the next chapter, leads to transition and a new season in our lives.

Chapter Five

Betrayal

And Judas, who betrayed Him, also knew the place;
for Jesus often met there with His disciples.

—John 18:2

etrayal is the most insidious form of emotional trauma that a person can experience. If you have ever been betrayed by someone close to you, you know the extreme pain that betrayal can cause in your heart, mind, and spirit. Betrayal can break your heart more quickly and more deeply than any other kind of emotional pain or trauma. It is much worse when the person is a brother- or sister-in-the-Lord.

Jesus suffered betrayal at the hands of one of the disciples, Judas. He sold Jesus out for thirty pieces of silver!

> *Then one of the twelve, called Judas Iscariot, went to the chief priests and said, "What are you willing to give me if I deliver Him to you?" And they counted out to him thirty pieces of silver.*
>
> (Matthew 26:14-15)

This betrayal preceded the transition in Jesus' ministry to his death and resurrection. It was necessary for God's plan of salvation to be accomplished and it was prophesied in Psalm 41 and Zechariah 11.

> *Even my own familiar friend in whom I trusted, who ate my bread, has lifted up his heel against me.*
>
> (Psalm 41:9)

> *Then I said to them, "If it is agreeable to you, give me my wages; and if not, refrain." So they weighed out for my wages thirty pieces of silver.*
>
> (Zechariah 11:12)

In spite of the fact that He knew it would happen, I believe that Jesus suffered the emotional pain of that betrayal. In Matthew 26:24, Jesus said,

> *"The Son of Man indeed goes just as it is written of Him, but woe to that man by whom the Son of Man is betrayed! It would have been good for that man if he had not been born."*

What a powerful statement! "It would have been good for that man if he had not been born." I think that the Lord takes betrayal *very* seriously and as followers of Jesus Christ, we need to do the same.

That is just one form of betrayal, delivering someone to an enemy. Betrayal can take other forms such as revealing confidential information or breaking a vow or a promise. It is always based in deception, which is lying. Since Satan is described as the father of lies in the Bible, we know that he and his army are at the root of betrayal. This is clearly pointed out in the following verses.

52

*Then Satan entered Judas, surnamed Iscariot, who
was numbered among the twelve. So he went his way
and conferred with the chief priests and captains, how
he might betray Him to them.*

(Luke 22:3-4)

As in this case, betrayal can be used by the kingdom of darkness
to bring disunity in ministries. Disunity is one trap that I discuss
further in chapter eleven. Many families and marriages have been
devastated as a result of betrayal. The Body of Christ is under attack
from the kingdom of darkness. When Christians betray and attack
each other, they are assisting the devil and his forces.

A lack of integrity within the Body of Christ has led to
backstabbing that resembles what occurs with non-Christians. This
practice is definitely not—loving one another—as Jesus instructed
His disciples. Gossip is extremely damaging and often results from
broken promises of confidentiality. That betrayal can and has caused
unimaginable emotional pain for those who were betrayed in this way.

All-too-common, overwhelming heartbreak occurs when people
are serving the Lord Jesus and being productive for God's kingdom
only to be attacked and gossiped about by fellow Christians. The
ones doing this do not realize how much pain they are inflicting on
others in the Body of Christ. It may be done out of jealousy or pride,
but it is always sin and causes deep wounds to those who are the
targets of the betrayal. Many of those who were betrayed have left the
Church as a result. *Thank God* that Jesus is able to heal those hurts
and release that pain!

Broken trust is always involved in betrayal. Whether it entails
disloyalty, unfaithfulness, infidelity, or any other form, trust is always
broken!

In chapter one, I shared the experience of my engagement to and
breakup with Al. What I need to add in this chapter is that while we
were engaged and before he became so ill, Al betrayed me by having

sex with a "friend" and coworker of mine. Al and I would sometimes give Lucy (not her real name) a ride home from work. One night, Al dropped me off at my house first and then took Lucy home. She invited him in. They had a few drinks and one thing led to another. When Al told me about this betrayal, I was heartbroken. However, I did not break our engagement because of his unfaithfulness. Even though I did not know Jesus as my *personal* Lord and Savior at that time, I knew about forgiveness and I chose to forgive Al. The emotional pain was still in my heart, but I did not allow myself to become bitter as a result of this broken trust and betrayal.

When my ex-husband was emotionally and physically abusing me, the feeling of betrayal was very real. I had trusted this man enough to marry him and I believed him when he told me that he loved me. The trust I had for him was betrayed on a large scale. At first, I blamed myself for not being a good enough wife as many women do, but I later realized that the abuse was not my fault at all. However, that did not lessen the emotional pain I carried for years as a result of this betrayal. Jesus released that pain over time through different types of healing ministry. *Praise the Lord!*

There are many examples in the Bible of situations where people went through various types of betrayal. Judas betrayed Jesus with a kiss (Matthew 26:49). Joseph was betrayed by his brothers and sold into slavery (Genesis 37:12-36). Delilah betrayed Samson after learning the secret to his strength. She had a man shave off Samson's hair and then turned him over to the Philistines for an enormous amount of money (Judges 16:4-21). Hosea's wife committed adultery (Hosea 3:1).

Adultery, breaking the marriage vows by having a sexual relationship with another person, is an extremely damaging form of betrayal. It destroys not only the trust between the married couple but also the soul of the one committing adultery.

Whoever commits adultery with a woman lacks understanding; He who does so destroys his own soul.
(Proverbs 6:32)

Ungodly soul ties are formed between the man and woman committing adultery. This negates the ability to be loyal to the godly soul ties with their spouse. The more the adultery is repeated, the more desensitized the people involved become as with any other sin. The ungodly soul ties become stronger and the result may be another marriage ended.

The Lord takes the marriage relationship so seriously that He calls it a "covenant" in Malachi 2:14. A *covenant* is the strongest form of faithfulness and commitment which acts like a guard over the marriage for blessings or judgment. When that covenant is broken, the righteous judgment of God is brought upon those guilty of breaking the marriage covenant.

One of the results of a broken marriage covenant is the decrease in love between the husband and wife. I believe this is God's judgment for one or both partners committing adultery. Jonathan Cahn made a very important statement during his address at the 2013 Inaugural Prayer Breakfast. He said, "There is no love without truth." Since deception is always involved any time adultery is committed, the love that should be between spouses suffers greatly when one of them commits adultery. That love continues to dwindle as the combination of betrayal and deception take on a life of its own. Usually, those committing adultery try to keep it hidden, but the Bible speaks about that as well. These are Jesus' words.

"For there is nothing covered that will not be revealed, nor hidden that will not be known."
(Luke 12:2)

This form of betrayal, adultery, can and often does lead to a transition in people's lives. Joan Hunter wrote in her book, *Healing the Heart, Overcoming Betrayal in Your Life*, about the emotional pain and physical issues she suffered as a result of her husband's infidelity. In this case, the betrayal led to divorce—a major transition in Joan's life. However, Joan also wrote about how, after time and much healing, God turned things around for good.

In addition to adultery, having an *emotional affair*, getting your emotional needs met by someone who is not your spouse, is another shattering form of betrayal that can destroy a marriage. An emotional affair between a married person and someone who is not their spouse also forms ungodly soul ties, which were mentioned above. Emotional affairs often lead to adultery. Jesus said in Matthew 5:28, "But I say to you that whoever looks at a woman to lust for her has already committed adultery with her in his heart." In case we have forgotten in our society, "You shall not commit adultery," is still one of the Ten Commandments!

In Matthew 24:10, while speaking about what things would be like just before His return, Jesus said, "And then many will be offended, will betray one another, and will hate one another." In Mark 13, Jesus also said,

> *"Now brother will betray brother to death, and a father his child; and children will rise up against parents and cause them to be put to death. And you will be hated by all for My name's sake. But he who endures to the end shall be saved."*
>
> (Mark 13:12-13)

This same warning was also reported in Matthew 10:21-22 and Matthew 24:9-13. Jesus knew that betrayal would be a significant issue during the end times and He warned us about it in His Word. He also gave us the answer to how we should react when we are betrayed. Jesus said that we need to *love our enemies*!

> *"But I say to you, love your enemies, bless those who*
> *curse you, do good to those who hate you, and pray*
> *for those who spitefully use you and persecute you,"*
> (Matthew 5:44)

Nowhere did Jesus say that we have to trust someone to love them. He also did not say that we have to continue in relationship with them. If the person is not remorseful and repentant, we should not stay in the relationship unless the Lord leads us to do so knowing the possibility of future reconciliation. If they honestly repent and/or seek help to stop the behavior, we should cautiously and with the Lord's direction, support their pursuing freedom from the sin. However, allowing them to continue to hurt and abuse us with their betrayal and deception is *not* how the Lord wants us to live. We must value ourselves as sons and daughters of the Most High God who loves us beyond anything we can imagine. It grieves Him when we don't set godly boundaries with people.

Also, loving the person "heaps coals of fire" on them and the Lord will reward you for obeying Him. The conviction of the Lord is more powerful than anything we could possibly do in return.

> *If your enemy is hungry, give him bread to eat; and*
> *if he is thirsty, give him water to drink; for so you*
> *will heap coals of fire on his head, and the LORD will*
> *reward you.*
> (Proverbs 25:21-22)

This was repeated by the Apostle Paul in Romans 12:20. In verse 21, Paul said, "Do not be overcome by evil, but overcome evil with good." Retaliation is *never* the answer for a follower of Jesus Christ.

I am not saying that this is easy. I have personally experienced incredible amounts of betrayal by others in my life. I will not discuss specifics, but I will say that I know firsthand how devastating it is to be betrayed by another follower of Jesus Christ. At times, it shook me right to the core, but I always ran to the Lord. He is always faithful and will never betray us. *Praise the Lord!*

Surviving and healing from betrayal requires a level of obedience to God that comes through years of training in His school of life. Forgiving someone that has betrayed us is the most difficult thing to do. It may require that you receive inner healing ministry prayer from another believer. If you allow the pain to fester inside you, it will turn into bitterness and resentment. In time, it will also affect you physically. Dealing with these emotional hurts is for *your* benefit and well-being. It is absolutely necessary if we are going to "endure to the end."

We must prepare our own hearts by dealing with the pain from betrayals and other trauma in order to fulfill the destiny that the Most High God has planned for us. The next chapter discusses more about heart preparation.

> *Draw near to God and He will draw near to you.*
> *Cleanse your hands, you sinners; and purify your*
> *hearts, you double-minded.*
>
> (James 4:8)

Chapter Six

Preparing Your Own Heart

Create in me a clean heart, O God,
and renew a steadfast spirit within me.

—Psalm 51:10

E ntering into inner healing ministry is a blessing as well as an incredible challenge personally. Unforgiveness, anger, bitterness, resentment, emotional pain, and/or trauma that are hidden in your own heart *will* come to the surface. The Lord is merciful and will allow us to minister His healing and deliverance in spite of our hidden inner issues for a time, but eventually He will give us the opportunity to reach new levels of personal freedom.

As we minister to others, our past hurts will eventually emerge and they will greatly hinder our ability to minister, or they will end up taking us out of ministry altogether, unless we receive the necessary healing. We all need inner healing to some extent. It is available to us because of the price that Jesus paid on the cross and His glorious resurrection!

But we all, with unveiled face, beholding as in a
mirror the glory of the Lord, are being transformed
into the same image from glory to glory, just as by the
Spirit of the Lord.

(2 Corinthians 3:18)

Inner healing is a *process* and I do not believe that anyone ever attains perfection and complete wholeness on this earth. That happens when we get to heaven. As we continue to live in this world, new emotional pain and trauma come our way. It is inevitable. No one has a pain-free life. Some have had more of these unwanted experiences than others but we are all subjected to emotional pain and trauma at one time or another. However, as the Lord reveals things in us that need to be healed, we are responsible to seek out that healing. It is a lifelong process. As the level of healing increases in us, the closer to the Lord we can become. Hearing Him becomes easier and that is a necessity if we are going to help others obtain freedom.

> *Search me, O God, and know my heart; Try me, and know my anxieties;*
>
> (Psalm 139:23)

This is why we have required that anyone interested in our Intern/ Training Program go through as many sessions as necessary of *Healing the Brokenhearted Ministry* before beginning the program. When you observe a ministry recipient receiving inner healing prayer, emotional pain in your own heart can be triggered. I know. This has happened to me on a few occasions. Trainees have also experienced their own emotional pain coming to the surface during a session at times. We may think that all of our emotional or spiritual wounds have been dealt with, but when we hear about someone else's life journey of pain and trauma, if there is a similarity to ours and the pain has not been healed and released, we will know it.

The first time this happened to me was during a *Healing the Brokenhearted Ministry* session with a woman who had adopted her son. As she talked about some of the painful things that had taken place with him, I felt painful emotions in my own heart that I thought were healed. Obviously, they were not. Therefore, as soon as I could deal with that pain, I prayed and Jesus released it from me. This was another layer of freedom for me personally. I now know that specific area has been healed because I have subsequently ministered to other women who had adopted children and the pain was no longer in my heart. *Praise the Lord!*

> *"So God, who knows the heart, acknowledged them by giving them the Holy Spirit, just as He did to us, and made no distinction between us and them, purifying their hearts by faith."*
>
> (Acts 15:8-9)

So, it is not necessarily a bad thing when painful emotions are triggered in us. It is an opportunity for the Lord to do another level of healing in our hearts. His timing is perfect and He knows when we can go through a new level of healing. Jesus is a Gentleman and will never give us more than we can handle with Him by our side. If emotional pain is being triggered in you, take the opportunity to seek help in receiving the inner healing and freedom that you need.

> *And Joshua said to the people, "Sanctify yourselves, for tomorrow the LORD will do wonders among you."*
>
> (Joshua 3:5)

Sanctifying ourselves also includes *spiritual cleansing.* Cleansing in the spiritual realm is just as necessary for a born-again Christian as taking a bath or shower is necessary in the physical realm. Most people would not bathe just once in their lives and expect to continue to be clean. In the same way, we need to cleanse ourselves spiritually on a regular basis. We live in a world in which evil and darkness abound. We must, therefore, be diligent about doing some very basic cleansing in the spiritual realm to rid ourselves of spiritual contamination that can build up and interfere with our relationship with God and our peace. As born-again believers in Jesus Christ, we have the authority to appropriate the blood of Jesus on our behalf to return to a place of peace within our spirits and souls.

This also applies to deliverance and spiritual warfare. We cannot expect to go through a deliverance session one time and be "good to go" for the rest of our lives. We are exposed to demonic and evil spirits on a daily basis in the fallen world in which we live. As long as the devil thinks he has a right to send his helpers our way to torment and oppress us, he will. He attempted to do it personally to Jesus. Why should we think we are exempt from demonic oppression?

> *Now when the devil had ended every temptation, he departed from Him* (Jesus) *until an opportune time.*
> (Luke 4:13, clarification added)

The Bible says that the devil walks about like a roaring lion seeking whom he may devour (1 Peter 5:8). It also says that his job is to steal, to kill, and to destroy (John 10:10). He will do everything he can to destroy a Christian, and we must be persistent in pursuing our freedom from things that allow the devil to oppress us. The devil is a legalist and will take advantage of anything from our past that we have not been cleansed from as an open door and entry point into our daily lives.

Deliverance is a process that can include confessing sin, repenting for past involvement in ungodly practices, breaking ungodly soul ties, breaking generational curses, and removing the demonic spirits that have been tormenting us for years. It includes prayer to release us from things that bind us and keep us from fulfilling our destiny. Deliverance can also occur spontaneously as past pain and trauma are released from our hearts. If done by a trained and qualified follower of Jesus Christ, it will not harm the ministry recipient in any way.

Deliverance should not be a process to fear but a blessing through which people attain a higher level of freedom in Jesus. The Bible includes many passages regarding deliverance.

> *"Heal the sick, cleanse the lepers, raise the dead, **cast out demons**."*
>
> (Matthew 10:8, emphasis added)

> *Then the seventy returned with joy, saying, "Lord, even the demons are subject to us in Your name." And He said to them, "I saw Satan fall like lightning from heaven. Behold, I give you the authority to trample on serpents and scorpions, and over all the power of the enemy, and nothing shall by any means hurt you. Nevertheless do not rejoice in this, that the spirits are subject to you, but rather rejoice because your names are written in heaven."*
>
> (Luke 10:17-20)

> *He who is in you is greater than he who is in the world.*
>
> (1 John 4:4)

However, there is also a serious warning in Acts 19 about trying to do deliverance when your heart and spirit are not right with the Lord. Please take this seriously. It is the reason that we must cleanse ourselves as much as possible before we enter into any kind of ministry to emotionally and spiritually wounded people.

> *Then some of the itinerant Jewish exorcists took it upon themselves to call the name of the Lord Jesus over those who had evil spirits, saying, "We exorcise you by the Jesus whom Paul preaches." Also there*

*were seven sons of Sceva, a Jewish chief priest, who
did so. And the evil spirit answered and said, "Jesus
I know, and Paul I know; but who are you?" Then
the man in whom the evil spirit was leaped on them,
overpowered them, and prevailed against them, so
that they fled out of that house naked and wounded.*
(Acts 19:13-16)

This is an example of spiritual warfare where there were casualties due to ignorance. The Bible includes numerous Scriptures describing spiritual warfare. Spiritual warfare is just that—*warfare*! It is very real. It is not a game. It is also not a onetime battle that we fight and then have victory for the rest of our lives. The enemy will fight Christians tooth and nail all of their lives. That is why we are instructed in the Bible to use the weapons that the Lord has provided to protect ourselves from the attacks of the enemy. We would not need these weapons if we were not in a real battle!

*Put on the whole armor of God, that you may be able
to stand against the wiles of the devil.*
(Ephesians 6:11)

I will discuss several of my spiritual warfare experiences in the next chapter. For this discussion, a basic definition of spiritual warfare is *applying the authority of the name and the shed blood of the Lord Jesus Christ to counteract demonic activity according to biblical principles.* Not only are the devil and his demonic forces out to make a Christian's life miserable, but many of those who practice the occult seriously are also involved in sending attacks our way. Witches, Satanists, witchdoctors, and other occultists pray fervently to their gods, all of whom are the devil or his cohorts. There is power in their prayers and they can be damaging to a believer's life.

Knowledge in these matters can help us in the battle but should never cause us to be afraid.

> *My people are destroyed for lack of knowledge.*
>
> (Hosea 4:6)

> *"No weapon formed against you shall prosper, and every tongue which rises against you in judgment you shall condemn. This is the heritage of the servants of the LORD, and their righteousness is from Me," says the LORD.*
>
> (Isaiah 54:17)

This does not mean that we should become experts or focus on the practices of those involved in the occult unless the Lord specifically calls us to do so.

It is much more beneficial for us to dwell on the things of the Lord. The Bible tells us to mediate on things that are true, noble, just, pure, lovely, of good report, of virtue, and praiseworthy (Philippians 4:8). Recent scientific studies have shown that reading God's Word out loud actually helps to rewire our brains. The Lord knows what is best for us to receive healing in every area. *Praise God!*

There are specific things we can do and pray regularly to be better protected from the attacks of the kingdom of darkness. The following basic steps will help you in your journey to a more peaceful and joyous walk with the Lord Jesus Christ. Remember, do not fear. The King of kings and Lord of lords is with you! *Before you begin doing any spiritual cleansing, be sure that you have submitted your heart to God.*

> **Therefore submit to God.** *Resist the devil and he will flee from you.*
>
> (James 4:7, emphasis added)

You can pray the following prayer out loud—*from your heart*—to submit to God. Then, pray through the bulleted instructions for spiritual cleansing. Chapter twelve includes more detail about becoming a born-again Christian. However, you can pray this prayer right now to ask Jesus to become your *personal* Lord and Savior for the first time if you have never done so. There is never a better time than the present to ask Jesus Christ to come into your life!

> *"True Lord Jesus Christ, I believe that You died on the cross for my sins and rose again from the dead. I humbly ask You to be my personal Lord and Savior. You redeemed me by Your blood, and I belong to You. I thank You, True Lord Jesus, that I can be cleansed today through Your precious blood.*
>
> *I now confess and renounce all my sins, known and unknown. I ask You to forgive me, Father God, in the name of Your Son, Jesus Christ.*
>
> *I renounce every work of darkness with which I have been in agreement, and I ask You, Father God, to forgive me in the name of the True Lord Jesus Christ. I call upon You now, True Lord Jesus, to deliver me and set me free. All this I pray in the name of Jesus Christ of Nazareth. Thank You, Father God, and Thank You, True Lord Jesus. Amen."*

Do not continue with these bulleted instructions if you are *not* a Christian. Doing so would invite increased demonic oppression. If you are currently involved in a cult or occult practices or did so in the past, do *not* attempt to cleanse yourself without a qualified, experienced, Christian prayer minister to help you.

Otherwise, if you prayed the above prayer, continue regularly with the following basic steps for spiritual cleansing.

- Confess any sin and ask Father God to forgive you in the name of Jesus Christ. *Repent* by changing the way you think about that sin to see it as God does, and line up your heart with the heart of God. Invite the conviction of the Holy Spirit to change your mind and heart. As a result, your behavior will change to glorify God.

- Unforgiveness is a major block to spiritual freedom. Therefore, you must forgive anyone who has offended you. I discuss this in more detail in chapter eight. Forgive in obedience to the Lord and by an act of your will. You can do this by praying, "Father God, what (*insert the person's name*) did hurt me and the pain is real. However, I forgive them in obedience to Your Word, Lord, in Jesus' name." (*You may not feel like you have forgiven them until the pain is released through inner healing ministry.* If you feel that you are absolutely not able to forgive someone, pursue inner healing to release the pain and trauma.)

- Word curses are very frequently spoken over us intentionally and unintentionally by people, including ourselves. The Bible states that death and life are in the power of the tongue (Proverbs 18:21). Words that are spoken can and do impact our lives in real ways. You can break word curses by saying the following out loud, "I break all word curses spoken against me and command the attached demons to go to the dry place in the name of Jesus Christ. Holy Spirit, I ask you to fill the voids." The name of Jesus is above every other name!

- Demonic spirits can transfer from one person to another. I do not believe that they can possess a believer but they can hang around and cause us misery and torment. To cleanse yourself from transferred demonic spirits say out loud, "I command all transferred demonic spirits to leave me now and go to the dry place in Jesus' name. Holy Spirit, I ask you to fill the voids."

- Occultists can send assignments, curses, hexes, vexes, spells, incantations, and do blood sacrifices that can cause us much harm if we are not diligent in doing spiritual cleansing. To counteract things sent by them, pray out loud, "I command all assignments, curses, hexes, vexes, spells, incantations, blood sacrifices, and any other work of darkness sent to me to be broken in the name of Jesus Christ of Nazareth. I command all demons attached to those assignments, curses, hexes, vexes, spells, incantations, blood sacrifices, and any other work of darkness sent to me to go to the dry place in the name and on the authority of Jesus Christ. Holy Spirit, I ask You to fill the voids."

- Ask the Holy Spirit to fill you and wash over you every day. He wants to be invited to fill you.

- *Thank Jesus* when you are done! Thankfulness is essential in the healing process.

You may ask, "Why do you command the demons to go to the *dry place?*" As I have searched the Bible, I have only found a few references to the location where demons go when they are evicted. In Matthew 12:42, Jesus said, "When an unclean spirit goes out of a man, he goes through dry places, seeking rest, and finds none." Luke 11:24 repeats this statement. I believe that "dry places" refers to *spiritually* dry places, not necessarily arid geographic locations. I have found no biblical basis for commanding demons to go to the pit of hell. We must be careful not to overstep our authority! That *will* get us into trouble.

Many well-meaning Christians have also gotten themselves into trouble by being too zealous about wanting to serve the Lord without pursuing their own healing first. As a result, they have often ended up burned-out or beaten down so badly that they almost give up on God completely. There are numerous Christian inner healing ministries available to help believers receive the healing and freedom that Jesus' death and resurrection provided for us. *Healing the Brokenhearted Ministry* is one that has helped many men and women. The main thing is that you get *biblically* based help.

I have prayed with numerous women who have been at the point of severe discouragement and even despair by the time they contacted me for an appointment. Yet, they have been reaching out to friends and family either trying to lead them to the Lord, or praying with them about life situations. This desire to help others drained them. They had also picked up *secondary trauma* from their friends and family in their own hearts and spirits which was weighing them down.

Secondary trauma impacts our spirits even though we did not experience the traumatic event firsthand. Ministers, counselors, mental health professionals, police officers, firefighters, and people in many other professions that deal with the public can carry debilitating amounts of secondary pain and trauma. A lady who attended one of my seminars told me that she had to stop counseling due to the secondary pain and trauma that had built up in her. She had been a licensed counselor for many years. Jesus released that secondary pain and trauma during her prayer sessions with me.

We must also be diligent about releasing secondary pain and trauma after we minister to someone. Otherwise, it will build up in us and we will experience the pain that the ministry recipients had been carrying.

The prayer for releasing secondary pain and trauma is extremely effective. However, it must be done regularly to avoid the overwhelming effects of secondary trauma on our hearts and spirits. When I first began ministering HBH, I forgot about releasing the secondary trauma after just two sessions. The next day, I felt awful. I asked the Lord what was going on with me and He gently said, "You did not release the secondary trauma." I immediately prayed to release it and the terrible heaviness lifted. Again, just like bathing or showering is not a onetime thing, releasing secondary trauma must be done regularly to remain free from it.

Another aspect of spiritual cleansing involves the environment in which you live. In order for us as followers of Jesus Christ to live in as much peace and joy as possible, we must pray for spiritual cleansing in our home and on our property to get rid of spiritual oppression (demonic spirits) that may have come into our environment. Our homes should be a sanctuary from oppression from the kingdom of darkness and, just as we clean them in the physical realm, we need to clean them in the spiritual realm. The frequency that this is needed depends on who has been in your home and/or on your property and what has occurred there. For additional information, there is an excellent book available, *Spiritual Housecleaning*, and I have listed it in the resources section at the end of this book.

In addition to the above spiritual cleansing, you must pursue personal inner healing ministry. As followers of Jesus Christ, we can do a lot on our own but we need each other for the most effective healing and freedom. None of us is an island and being isolated is the best way to become a casualty in spiritual warfare. Sheep are devoured when the wolf finds them isolated and away from the rest of the flock. The devil does the same thing. If he can get Christians off by themselves, he is better able to be successful in his goals of stealing, killing, and destroying his enemies.

Be wise. Seek out help with someone that takes confidentiality seriously. Ask other Christians who they trust. Many have been hurt by a lack of confidentiality in the Body of Christ under the pretense of "I am just telling you so that you can pray for so-and-so." This is nothing less than gossip and has caused untold numbers of Christians to shy away from receiving the inner healing ministry they need. There are Christian counselors and ministers who can help you without divulging your personal business to everyone they know.

Don't let past experiences of being wounded by other Christians stop you from obtaining your inner healing and freedom! This has been part of Satan's strategy against the kingdom of God. It is just one piece of the puzzle in spiritual warfare but it is a major one. Don't let past or present attacks from the kingdom of darkness prevent you from preparing your own heart so that you can fulfill your God-given destiny!

Spiritual warfare can have a wide range of real––mild to intense and sometimes life-threatening––effects on people.

Chapter Seven

Spiritual Adversity...
Spiritual Warfare!

S piritual warfare is real. It is not a game. I cannot emphasize this enough! The devil is playing for keeps and he does not play fair. Denying the existence of the devil and spiritual warfare will only cause you to be a casualty in the war. We must be "wise as serpents and harmless as doves" (Matthew 10:16).

> *For we do not wrestle against flesh and blood, but against principalities, against powers, against the rulers of the darkness of this age, against spiritual hosts of wickedness in the heavenly places. Therefore take up the whole armor of God, that you may be able to withstand in the evil day, and having done all, to stand.*
>
> (Ephesians 6:12-13)

We must also learn to distinguish between spiritual warfare and the everyday trials that come our way in the natural realm. Every difficulty that we encounter is not a result of spiritual warfare. Discerning the difference takes years of experience and training in the school of hard knocks. Knowing the telltale signs of spiritual warfare make it easier to recognize interference in our life from the kingdom of darkness. However, as we "fight the good fight," we need to remember that the Lord tells us that we are not to be afraid!

Fear not, for I am with you; be not dismayed, for I am your God. I will strengthen you, Yes, I will help you, I will uphold you with My righteous right hand.

(Isaiah 41:10)

The LORD is my light and my salvation; whom shall I fear? The LORD is the strength of my life; of whom shall I be afraid?

(Psalm 27:1)

For God has not given us a spirit of fear, but of power and of love and of a sound mind.

(2 Timothy 1:7)

Many of the incidents of spiritual warfare that we have encountered through the years could have very easily caused us to react in fear. Some of them did throw us a little off balance for short periods of time, but standing firm on the foundation of Jesus Christ kept us from giving in to Satan's plan. When the devil uses other people, especially Christians, in his attacks, the results can be particularly painful.

Other people are not the main source of the spiritual adversity and warfare in our lives but they can definitely be used, knowingly or unknowingly, by the devil and his army. Peter was one vessel that the enemy tried to use against Jesus. When Peter told Jesus that what He was saying about His coming suffering, death, and resurrection would not happen, Jesus replied sharply.

*But He turned and said to Peter, "Get behind Me,
Satan! You are an offense to Me, for you are not
mindful of the things of God, but the things of men."*
(Matthew 16:23)

Jesus recognized that Satan was using Peter's mouth to come
against Him. It is the same today when the devil speaks though our
own family, friends, or others. I have experienced this tactic more
than once over the past twenty-seven years. When Bob and I were
planning to remodel the garage and had applied for the business
license, the devil, or one of his helpers, spoke through someone very
close to me at the time and said, "You will never get that license!" As
a new believer and extremely inexperienced in the area of spiritual
warfare, my reaction was to cry. The words had come through the
mouth of a person that had a lot of influence in my life, and I could
not believe they would say such a hurtful and discouraging thing.
After praying about it, I later understood that the words were coming
from the enemy and the human being was being used as his pawn.
The devil does not play fair!

Of course, we did get the business license and the whole situation
was meant to discourage me and get my focus on the person and off
what the Lord was telling us to do. *Thank God*, it did not work! People
often do not realize how they are being manipulated by the enemy
in spiritual warfare but, many times, they do know exactly what the
enemy is doing through them.

The following is a great example of spiritual warfare through a
person. I received a phone call at the bookstore about a week before
a Christian concert, which we were sponsoring in Los Alamos. The
man on the other end of the line wanted to know if we sold the Bible. I
said, "Yes, we sell the Holy Bible." He then asked if we had the "King
David Bible." Since that is not a version of the Bible, I assumed that
he was a new Christian and confused about the King James Version

of the Bible. So, I explained that we had several versions of the Bible in stock including the King James Version (KJV).

To better help this man, I asked what church he attended because that could give me a clue about what Bible version would be appropriate for his use. When he replied that he attended one of the Wiccan covens in the area, I was surprised to say the least. I said, "You attend a coven and you want a Holy Bible?" He said, "Yes," and wanted to know if it would burn. I went along with him and calmly told him that I was sure it would burn since all of the Bibles we had in stock were made of paper. Then, this obviously deceived man asked how much the King James Bible would cost. I explained that we had several types in stock but I quoted him the price for the most expensive, leather-bound, KJV Bible that I had available. Next, he started swearing, using the Lord's name as a curse word, and told me that I "must be possessed." Of course, he hung up right after that. Wow! I was stunned that we had stirred up the kingdom of darkness to that extent. We were doing something right. *Praise the Lord!*

That man knew what he was doing and he was playing right into Satan's hands. Thankfully, it did not have the desired effect of deterring us from the path we were on. Over 800 people attended that concert. It was the largest Christian concert held in Los Alamos' history and over a hundred people responded to the invitation to ask Jesus to be their personal Lord and Savior. *Praise God!*

Another time, early one morning after arriving at the bookstore, I noticed that there was a message on the answering machine. This was not unusual but the message certainly was from the kingdom of darkness. A man's voice said, "Which church would burn the best?" This was not even remotely funny since one of the local churches had suffered considerable damage a few weeks earlier as the result of arson. I immediately called the police who took the cassette tape as evidence and followed up on the threat.

When we opened the bookstore, I thought that it would be such a blessing, and in untold ways it was, but the spiritual warfare we encountered was completely unexpected. The enemy used non-Christians as well as Christians to perpetrate his attacks. However, the Lord helped us every step of the way and we learned volumes as a result. I now realize that we were in training for the spiritual warfare that would be coming our way in subsequent years.

As the years passed, the spiritual warfare due to the bookstore increased exponentially. Things really heated up when the Lord directed us to stock the book, *Wicca: Satan's Little White Lie*. Several local Wiccans came into the store. One purchased the book telling the girl on duty, "I just want to see what the opposition is saying about us." He came back quite often and walked around the store. We prayed and anointed the store and each other after he left every time. It is *warfare*!

One day, a woman from Santa Fe came into the bookstore and wrote a check in the amount of the Wicca book's cost. I asked the girl who was working if she remembered what that lady had purchased because I also noticed that a copy of the Wicca book had been sold. The employee remembered the lady very well and verified that was the book she bought. What had gotten my attention was a pagan symbol on the woman's check. So, I paid close attention to her name. I will call her Louise Jones (not her real name).

Approximately a week later, an irate woman entered the bookstore. She was demanding a refund for the Wicca book. The employee on duty was a mature lady who tried to calm the woman down. She explained that we did not give cash refunds as was stated on our receipts. This woman who gave the employee a suspiciously odd, occult-sounding name said that she was a practicing Wiccan and a friend had given her the book. She said that she was highly offended and wanted a refund. Again, the manager told her that she would be happy to exchange the book or give her a store credit. The Wiccan lady decided to have us give the credit to a friend of hers, Lucy (not her real name). She gave us Lucy's phone number and then left the store. What transpired after that was even more bizarre.

I called Lucy and introduced myself. After I explained the situation and that her friend wanted her to have the store credit, Lucy told me that she did not know anyone by *that* name. She asked me to describe the lady and, when I did, she exclaimed, "That sounds like my friend, Louise Jones!" Lucy said that she was *sure* Louise was not a Wiccan because she had been visiting her church with her. When I asked what church she attended, Lucy said that she was a member of the Mormon Church. Then, Lucy got angry and started rebuking me for not being a "loving" Christian and for selling things that were hurtful to people of other religions. She told me that she did not want the store credit and hung up on me. This explained a lot. Louise Jones was the woman who had purchased the Wicca book a week before and the same woman who returned it. She had obviously used her Wiccan name when she came back and tried to get a refund.

I already felt like I was in the twilight zone but things got even worse. Fifteen minutes earlier, when Louise had left the book in the store, I did not realize what was going on and I put that copy of the book back on the shelf. *Big mistake!* By the time I got off the phone with Lucy, I was physically ill. I had a headache, dizziness, and nausea. Our employee was also feeling sick and Bob, who had stopped in the store for a few minutes but was now back at work at LANL, was in the same shape. *The book!*

I anointed the store, myself, and our employee. Then I destroyed that book and removed the remains from the store. All of our physical symptoms disappeared! Bob anointed himself at work and his symptoms disappeared as well. The blood of Jesus is beyond anything that witchcraft or any other occult practice can do. *Praise the Lord!*

As in this example, spiritual warfare can have a wide range of real—mild to intense and sometimes life-threatening—effects on people. Once we sense that we are being impacted by some form of spiritual warfare, we need to pray and pray fervently. If we are unable to pray because the effect is too overwhelming for us, we must ask someone else to pray for us. We can also pray Scriptures over ourselves as in Psalm 91, especially verses five through eight.

> *You shall not be afraid of the terror by night, nor of the arrow that flies by day, nor of the pestilence that walks in darkness, nor of the destruction that lays waste at noonday. A thousand may fall at your side, and ten thousand at your right hand; but it shall not come near you. Only with your eyes shall you look, and see the reward of the wicked.*
>
> (Psalm 91:5-8)

Remember, if we give in to fear, we are giving the enemy an upper hand. Another thing that we must be careful not to do in this spiritual war is overstep our authority. In Jude 9, it says that Michael, the archangel, in contending with the devil, *dared not* bring a reviling accusation against him. Many believers have gotten themselves in hot water, so to speak, by coming against the devil himself or against the principality realm, and they have experienced major retaliation as a result. There are appropriate biblical protocol for asking God to send war angels to battle principalities and even the devil. *Be careful!*

I mentioned this in the last chapter but it bears repeating. We should all learn a lesson from the seven sons of Sceva who got themselves into major trouble by using the name of Jesus inappropriately. The name of Jesus is not some guarantee of limitless power against demons or the kingdom of darkness. It must be applied by a born-again Christian who is walking with the Lord to the best of their ability. Any known sin is an open door for the enemy to retaliate. Remember, the devil is a legalist and will take advantage of anything possible in this war. The seven sons of Sceva experienced the harsh reality of spiritual warfare.

And the evil spirit answered and said, "Jesus I know, and Paul I know; but who are you?" Then the man in whom the evil spirit was leaped on them, overpowered them, and prevailed against them, so that they fled out of that house naked and wounded.

(Acts 19:15-16)

In Luke 10:19, Jesus said, "Behold, I give you the authority to trample on serpents and scorpions, and over all the power of the enemy, and nothing shall by any means hurt you." Jesus said that he gave His disciples authority over all the *power* of the enemy, *not* over the enemy. We do not have the authority to command Satan or evil beings in high places, principalities for example, to do anything.

Jesus never cast Satan into hell, nor did He prevent him from operating in the spiritual realm. When Satan was tempting Jesus in the wilderness as reported in Matthew 4:10, Jesus said, "Away with you, Satan!" Luke 4:13 says that Satan then "departed from Him until an opportune time." Also, in Matthew 16:23, Jesus said, "Get behind Me, Satan!" Now, if Jesus Christ, the Son of God, did not send Satan into the pit of hell, why should Christians think they have the authority to do so? We don't! According to the Word of God, Satan will be sent there in the end after Jesus returns to this earth (Revelation 20:10).

Within my level of authority in Jesus Christ, the Lord has given me a supernatural boldness at times that I could never have imagined. As I said in chapter two, selling the Wicca book did not come without a cost to us personally. One day, one of the Wiccan high priestesses in the area came into the bookstore absolutely livid after I had left to go home. The manager on duty called me after the woman left the store to inform me that she had made an appointment for me to meet with the lady the following morning. I thanked her for the warning and called several prayer warriors, enlisting their help in the spiritual realm.

The spiritual warfare had ramped up another level. Upon arriving at the store the next morning, we anointed ourselves and the store with oil in anticipation of the battle to come. However, the prayers were already being answered and the Wiccan high priestess, Ellen (not her real name), was delayed for several hours due to problems at work. When she got to the bookstore, she was visibly tired. She, the bookstore manager, and I went into the back room to talk. The couch she was sitting on had been anointed with oil that morning, and I trusted that the Lord was in control. The Lord filled me with an amazing amount of peace and boldness. Ellen began to present her case requesting that I stop selling the Wicca book. I listened and responded to each argument with the Holy Spirit's leading.

> *And when they had prayed, the place where they had assembled together was shaken; and they were all filled with the Holy Spirit, and they **spoke the word of God with boldness**.*
>
> (Acts 4:31, emphasis added)

Ellen offered to write a pamphlet that I could give out to those who wanted to know about Wicca. She said that the Wicca book was full of lies and that she was an expert on her religion. I was also aware that she had presented Wicca at the high school humanities class. The Lord had me answer her by saying that I could not give out material that said witchcraft was okay since I sold the Holy Bible that says it is an abomination to the Lord. Deuteronomy 18:12 actually says that *all who do these things*, including practicing witchcraft, *are an abomination to the Lord*. I believe that the Holy Spirit allowed me to misquote that Scripture to avoid additional arguments and to keep the atmosphere under control. The woman responded, "I understand." I also told her that I would not stop selling the book, and that I trusted the Christian author since we were in unity in Jesus Christ. She warned me in a roundabout way that our discussion would not be the end of the contact. Then she left peacefully.

The next day, the spiritual warfare went to an even higher level. I received a letter in the mail from the high priest of the same coven to which Ellen belonged. After I opened the letter, I immediately prayed and called some prayer warriors for their assistance. The letter explained that the coven would take us to court and sue us and the bookstore if we did not stop selling the Wicca book. They claimed that we were defaming their religion by having it in stock and making it available to the public. It was on letterhead stationery and quite official. I did not panic. Nevertheless, I did call a couple of attorneys and asked for their opinion. One attorney in Santa Fe said, "No judge in the country would give the lawsuit the time of day." Nothing further ever developed from that threat. *Praise the Lord!*

> *"Do not say, 'A conspiracy,' concerning all that this people call a conspiracy, nor be afraid of their threats, nor be troubled."*
>
> (Isaiah 8:12)

> *But thus says the LORD… "For I will contend with him who contends with you,"*
>
> (Isaiah 49:25)

Not all spiritual warfare is that overt and easily identified. In fact, most of it is rather subtle—but nevertheless just as effective—if it is not recognized for what it is. Delayed answer to prayer can be one example of this. Sometimes Christians take unanswered prayer as an indication that God is saying no. However, there is a perfect example in the Bible of spiritual warfare and how it can cause the answer to prayer to be delayed. We know from God's Word that Daniel was a serious man of prayer. He risked his own life to be obedient to God in prayer. Still, spiritual warfare interfered with the answer to his prayer as related in the following verses.

> *Then he said to me, "Do not fear, Daniel, for from*
> *the first day that you set your heart to understand,*
> *and to humble yourself before your God, your words*
> *were heard; and I have come because of your words.*
> *But the prince of the kingdom of Persia withstood*
> *me twenty-one days; and behold, Michael, one of the*
> *chief princes, came to help me, for I had been left*
> *alone there with the kings of Persia."*
>
> (Daniel 10:12-13)

Daniel had been praying and fasting before this encounter. The principality over the area was blocking the answer to his prayers and it required the assistance of the archangel Michael for the spiritual warfare victory to be accomplished. Principalities are extremely powerful and controlling forces in the kingdom of darkness. Their power is reinforced by those who are practicing sin and/or the occult. We must have a healthy understanding of this dynamic and use the correct biblical protocol when we pray regarding these types of strongholds.

Even though all the above are serious examples of spiritual warfare, the most effective and subtle warfare occurs in our minds. That is why the Bible exhorts us in 2 Corinthians 10:5 to take every thought captive. Many Christians are not too discerning when it comes to thoughts that appear in their minds. Thoughts can be our own, from the Holy Spirit, or from a demonic source. One test is whether or not the thought lines up with the Word of God. If you are still unsure about the source of a thought, you can also ask Jesus Christ to silence every voice that is not from Him.

Learning to distinguish the source of a thought is crucial in order for us to be victorious in the battle with the devil. This comes with years of training in the Lord's school of spiritual warfare. Experience is the best teacher. Be patient with yourself. The Lord is merciful and gracious, and He uses all things for our good!

Often when I am experiencing intense spiritual warfare in my mind, I feel like I am in a pressure cooker that is about to explode, in a fruit press, or in a vise. That is how I know personally that the enemy has turned up the heat and is desperately trying to break my resistance. It is not a pleasant or comfortable feeling but it always sends me to my knees in prayer. The Lord is faithful to relieve the pressure every time. *Thank You, Jesus!*

Paul described in the following verses how I have felt numerous times during and after an intense attack of spiritual warfare.

> *We are hard-pressed on every side, yet not crushed;*
> *we are perplexed, but not in despair; persecuted, but*
> *not forsaken; struck down, but not destroyed——*
> (2 Corinthians 4:8-9)

As we pray with Christians for their freedom and healing, the spiritual warfare can be extreme and relentless. The devil does not want the Body of Christ to be free to serve the Lord and do damage to the kingdom of darkness, his kingdom. He fights inner healing ministry like no other. If you feel called to help those who are carrying pain and trauma, be forewarned——the battle is *ferocious.* Yes, the battle belongs to the Lord but we are His soldiers. As soldiers, we must consecrate all areas of our lives to our Lord Jesus and stay alert and watchful.

> *This charge I commit to you, son Timothy, according*
> *to the prophecies previously made concerning you,*
> *that by them you may wage the good warfare,*
> (1 Timothy 1:18)

No one engaged in warfare entangles himself with the
affairs of this life, that he may please him who enlisted
him as a soldier.

(2 Timothy 2:4)

Keep in mind that the Lord commands us to be strong. He also provides the strength we need. He commands us not to fear the enemy, and He promises that He will always be with us. *Praise the Lord!*

"Be strong and of good courage, do not fear nor be
afraid of them; for the LORD your God, He is the
One who goes with you. He will not leave you nor
forsake you."

(Deuteronomy 31:6)

"Have I not commanded you? Be strong and of good
courage; do not be afraid, nor be dismayed, for the
LORD your God is with you wherever you go."

(Joshua 1:9)

Prayer is talking to God
and listening for His response.
Many people talk to God but do not listen
or give Him the time to respond.

Chapter Eight

Increased Prayer is Essential

S piritual warfare is not something to be taken lightly. It is continuous, and the early church learned quickly that to survive and be victorious in the intense warfare, prayer had to be continuous. Being involved in ministering inner healing to those who have been emotionally, physically, mentally, spiritually, and/or sexually abused requires an amount of prayer coverage way beyond a normal prayer life.

> *but we will give ourselves continually to prayer and to the ministry of the word.*
>
> (Acts 6:4)

There is nothing wrong with praying a simple prayer in the morning or before going to sleep at night, but if that is the only prayer life you have, you are being denied a wonderful relationship with the Father, His Son, and the Holy Spirit. Developing a prayer life that lines up with 1 Thessalonians 5:17, which says, "Pray without ceasing," takes practice and determination. Not only is it essential for Christians in ministry, but it is also very beneficial for any believer who desires a deeper relationship with the Lord.

Be anxious for nothing, but in everything by prayer and supplication, with thanksgiving, let your requests be made known to God; and the peace of God, which surpasses all understanding, will guard your hearts and minds through Christ Jesus.

(Philippians 4:6-7)

Prayer is talking to God and listening for His response. Many people talk to God but do not listen or give Him the time to respond. Our relationship with Him is deepened in our prayer times. The more we talk to Him, respecting who He is and how merciful He has been to us, the more we can hear His voice. The Lord wants that kind of close communication with us. He wants us to be real with Him. He already knows everything about us and everything that is going on in our lives. However, He wants us to take the time to speak to Him about what concerns us and He wants us to take time to listen!

That does not mean that we have to be on our knees twenty-four hours a day to have this kind of close connection to God. Nevertheless, we can and should talk to Him all day long wherever we may be. I personally ask the Lord what He wants me to do each day whether I have specific plans or not. I ask the Lord when to go to certain places and even for a good parking spot when I get there. Since He knows all things, He knows much better than I do what accident, what traffic jam or what scheme of the Adversary may be avoided by listening to Him and following His instructions. As you increase the amount and quality of time you spend in prayer, it will become easier and feel normal for you to talk to the Lord "without ceasing."

You will keep him in perfect peace, whose mind is stayed on You, because he trusts in You.

(Isaiah 26:3)

A deeper prayer life also requires you to be extremely flexible and willing to change your plans to line up with the Lord's will. Keep in mind that He is well aware of our obligations and responsibilities and will never require us to become irresponsible or flighty to obey His instructions. It may very well require you to rearrange your daily plans but His plan is *always* the best one for us. I cannot count the number of times that I have totally changed my course of action to follow the Lord's plan.

Another result of increasing your prayer life is that you will be sensitized to the Lord's voice and hear Him talking to you when you least expect it. When we decided to remodel our garage and open the bookstore, it was because I had heard the Lord speaking to me while I was taking a shower. At the time, I was not in prayer, so to speak, and I was taken by surprise by the words I heard from Him. I wanted to be sure it was Him and began talking to Him about what I thought I heard. He gently confirmed that it was His voice. The rest is history.

In order to minister to people who are emotionally wounded and carrying unimaginable pain and trauma from the past, you must be able to clearly hear the Lord's voice and distinguish His voice from your thoughts and those of the enemy. This is important because God knows each person better than they do and He knows exactly what they need to be healed and set free. We may think we know what they need, but only the God of the Universe knows the perfect prescription for their recovery. Tuning our hearing to that level also takes practice and, since we are human, may involve being wrong at times. Do not be afraid that you will make a mistake. You may but God is totally able to take a mistake and correct the result through His grace and mercy.

The effective, fervent prayer of a righteous man avails much.

(James 5:16)

Again, you must be as free as possible yourself to avoid any interference with your prayers. Known sin will block our prayers from being heard and being answered by the Lord. As followers of Jesus Christ, we have the privilege of coming before the Father, asking for forgiveness for our sins, and receiving that forgiveness in Jesus' name. However, we must confess our sins to Him *and* repent.

> *But your iniquities have separated you from your God; and your sins have hidden His face from you, so that He will not hear.*
>
> (Isaiah 59:2)

> *What shall we say then? Shall we continue in sin that grace may abound? Certainly not! How shall we who died to sin live any longer in it?*
>
> (Romans 6:1-2)

Known sin in our lives can do more than block our prayers from being heard. It can also cause illness and other consequences to come upon us. We must go before the Lord and confess our sin and ask for His forgiveness when we are aware that we have sinned. Therefore, we must not continue in that sin. We must repent and "sin no more."

> *When Jesus had raised Himself up and saw no one but the woman, He said to her, "Woman, where are those accusers of yours? Has no one condemned you?" She said, "No one, Lord." And Jesus said to her, "Neither do I condemn you; **go and sin no more.**"*
>
> (John 8:10-11, emphasis added)

*Afterward Jesus found him in the temple, and said to him, "See, you have been made well. **Sin no more**, lest a worse thing come upon you."*

(John 5:14, emphasis added)

Repentance is not just saying *I repent*. It only happens when we are sincerely sorry for our sin and make an honest effort to walk away from that sin. It is conviction in your heart that you are guilty before God that leads to a change of mind about the sin which in turn leads to a change in behavior. The Bible says in 2 Corinthians 7:10, "For godly sorrow produces repentance leading to salvation, not to be regretted; but the sorrow of the world produces death." Just saying *I'm sorry* is not repentance either. It assures us that we will go around that same mountain again.

Therefore, to be able to have better communication with the Lord, repentance is essential. If you need help to obtain freedom from pain and trauma that are keeping you in a cycle of known sin, find it. You are responsible for what you know and if you know that what you are doing displeases God, you must do everything possible to receive freedom from that behavior. It is worth it to have a wonderful prayer life!

As I stated in chapter six, unforgiveness is an enormously powerful block to hearing the Lord and having the intimate relationship with Him that He desires for us. We must forgive everyone as an act of our will and in obedience to God. This does *not* let them off the hook for what they did but it releases us from the torment of carrying unforgiveness. It has been said that holding unforgiveness is like taking poison and expecting the other person to get sick. That does not happen. It can make us physically as well as emotionally sick, and it robs us of peace with God.

"And his master was angry, and delivered him to the torturers until he should pay all that was due to him.

So My heavenly Father also will do to you if each of you, from his heart, does not forgive his brother his trespasses."

(Matthew 18:34-35)

"And whenever you stand praying, if you have anything against anyone, forgive him, that your Father in heaven may also forgive you your trespasses. But if you do not forgive, neither will your Father in heaven forgive your trespasses."

(Mark 11:25-26)

Therefore, if you are carrying any unforgiveness, you can pray a simple prayer of forgiveness in obedience to the Lord. You may not *feel* like you have forgiven until the pain has been released from your heart which may require inner healing prayer with a trained Christian minister. In the meantime, it is vitally important that you pray to forgive those who have hurt you to the best of your ability. If you feel that you are absolutely *not able* to forgive someone, pursue inner healing to release the pain and trauma. Do whatever the Lord leads you to do in order to get free!

This is a sample prayer of forgiveness:

"Father God, what <u>(insert the person's name)</u> did to me hurt me a lot, and it still hurts today. However, as an act of obedience to Your will, I now choose to forgive him/her. I release him/her into Your hands. Father God, I also ask You to release the pain in my heart that I have from this situation. I willingly release it to you. Father, heal me and set me free. I pray this in the name of Your Son, the True Lord Jesus. Amen."

Once you have asked the Lord to forgive your sins and made the conscience decision to forgive all those who have hurt you, you will have a much easier time developing a closer and more fulfilling relationship with the Lord. Your communication with Him will be unhindered and the clarity with which you will hear His voice will significantly improve. The peace in your heart will also increase and there will be less legal ground for the enemy to attack you. This is all important in the maturing of your prayer life.

Another extremely important and indispensable aspect of ministering to those with wounded hearts is having a team of intercessors praying for you and your ministry. I cannot stress this enough. Without the prayer support of godly intercessors, the interference from and battle with the Adversary can become unnecessarily extreme and exhausting. Yes, we can pray individually and the Lord will hear our prayers as long as we have kept our hearts clean, but there is definitely additional power and strength in numbers.

When Herod imprisoned Peter and had a guard of sixteen soldiers watching him, the church was praying *constantly* for Peter.

> *Peter was therefore kept in prison, but constant prayer was offered to God for him by the church.*
>
> (Acts 12:5)

We know the result of that constant prayer by the church. Peter's chains fell off and an angel of the Lord escorted Peter out of the prison! This is just one example of the results of powerful, intercessory prayer in the Bible. However, if you pray for others, do not ask God to do anything that would violate their free will. He will not do that. Learn how to intercede according to God's Word.

"For My house shall be called a house of prayer for all nations."

(Isaiah 56:7)

The call of intercessor, someone who prays for other individuals, ministries, communities, and/or nations, is a precious gift to the rest of the Body of Christ. Without intercessors, those in ministry would have an extremely challenging and difficult time. I will be forever grateful to our intercessory team and the many hours that they sacrificially hold us and the ministry up in prayer. I know without a doubt that many of Satan's plans have been unsuccessful or dramatically less effective as a result of the prayers of our intercessors.

One example occurred on October 6, 2009. As Bob and I were on the way to minister in Albuquerque, we were involved in a five-car accident on the freeway. All the traffic was stopped on the ramp from one interstate road to another. However, seconds after we stopped in this traffic, a man driving a heavily loaded pickup truck that was three vehicles behind us waited too long to hit his brakes and, traveling at a high rate of speed, he plowed into the car in front of him. This pushed that car into the vehicle behind us causing that vehicle to crash into our van. We were then pushed into the car in front of us. In spite of all the damage to the vehicles involved, no one was critically injured, and the woman in the car hit by the truck was able to get out of her car on her own. *Praise the Lord!*

This accident happened one month before a two-day *Healing the Brokenhearted Ministry* seminar, which we had scheduled to take place in Albuquerque. I do not believe that it was a coincidence. It was an attempt by the Adversary to stop the seminar, thus preventing us from sharing about inner healing with those registered. Nevertheless, our injuries did not stop the seminar from happening as scheduled. There was an abundance of fruit for the Lord as a result. To the glory of God, Bob and I have both healed from the injuries to our necks, backs, and to my shoulder. I am convinced that our prayers and those of our intercessors prevented a much worse outcome.

Many of our intercessors pray with an unshakable determination and focus. They know the ministry's prayer needs and we keep them updated about our personal prayer needs as well. Intercessors always come before God on behalf of others. Moses was a great example of intercession that changed God's mind. Moses begged God not to destroy Israel and Israel was spared.

> *Then Moses pleaded with the LORD his God...So the LORD relented from the harm which He said He would do to His people.*
> (Exodus 32:11, 14)

Committed intercession is invaluable in spiritual warfare and sought after by God as shown in the next verse.

> *"So I sought for a man among them who would make a wall, and stand in the gap before Me on behalf of the land,"*
> (Ezekiel 22:30)

Intercessors "stand in the gap" as a link between individuals, families, ministries, cities, and nations to God's mercy. If you are thinking about becoming involved in ministering to those with broken hearts, seek out intercessors to pray for you and your family. The enemy does not like Christians getting set free from past pain and trauma, enabling them to fulfill their destiny and effectively serve the Lord. Satan and his army vigorously fight that from happening, and you need to have the prayers of as many intercessors as possible before, during, and after a ministry session.

Intercessory prayer coverage is one critical part of increased prayer when healing hearts is your goal. Another very significant component of increased prayer is becoming a person of praise and worship. Praise and worship are forms of prayer—communication with God. The more we praise God and thank Him for everything He is and has done for us, the more sensitive we become to His presence and voice. Therefore, to increase our intimacy with the Lord, we must tell Him daily how grateful we are for His love for us, for His Son, Jesus, and for the Holy Spirit. An attitude of thankfulness also helps in the healing process. Praising God has become second nature to me, and I do it every chance I get. We can never praise Him enough!

As we praise and worship the Lord, we are also doing spiritual warfare. Ezekiel 28:13 alludes to the fact that Satan was the praise and worship leader in heaven before his fall. The kingdom of darkness absolutely hates praise and worship. Demons flee when we worship the Lord in song or praise Him with words. When things get intense in the battle with the enemy, praise the Lord and watch the atmosphere change!

We can definitely change the atmosphere around us by praising and worshipping God. My following testimony is evidence of this.

At 5:00 am on August 31, 2009, the Lord woke me up and told me to go out on the back deck of the Apple Hill Lodge, where my husband and I were staying in Moravian Falls, North Carolina. An "open heaven" exists over Moravian Falls because it was established by the Moravian missionaries from the Herrnhut community in Germany who had people fasting, praying, and worshipping the Lord there twenty-four hours a day, seven days a week, for over one hundred years! We had been in Moravian Falls for several days attending a Gary and Kathi Oates' conference.

As I began taking pictures with my digital camera into the pitch-black darkness towards the apple orchard, the first forty to fifty photos were just that—completely black. I was determined to continue looking into the darkness for whatever the Lord had awakened me to see. I had been on this deck a year before and had an amazing, open-eyed vision and visitation of the Lord's presence there. So, I was not going to be easily discouraged and go back to bed.

While I waited, I started singing praise and worship songs, and as I did, angelic orbs began appearing in the photos! The more I sang, the more they came. When I would stop singing their numbers would decrease. As I sang *Alleluia,* they came quicker than during any other song. I took at least fifty photos that showed this angelic orb visitation as I sang and praised the Lord.

I believe that the orbs in these photos represent a supernatural manifestation of the presence of holy angels. The following five photos are a sampling of the photos I took that morning.

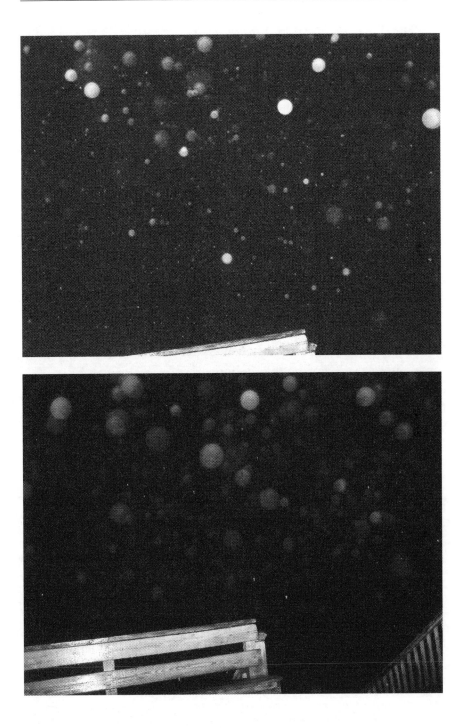

The best explanation I have found regarding these angelic orbs is by Max Greiner, a Christian sculptor with a background in photography. You can check it out at his website.

http://maxgreinerart.com/AngelOrbs.html

The Bible clearly instructs us not to worship angels. I am not suggesting that anyone do that. However, these amazing photos prove without a doubt that **praise changes the atmosphere!** So, *Praise the Lord!* As you do, you will increase your ability to connect to God and do battle against the kingdom of darkness at the same time.

I have also found that when people come for a ministry session, it helps immensely if they have spent a significant amount of time during the days prior to their appointment listening to praise and worship music. It prepares their hearts and spirits for what Jesus wants to heal in them, and they usually receive healing and freedom much more easily during the session.

It is essential that we increase our prayer life in any way possible in order to receive deeper levels of God's healing and to be able to pray for healing with others. We cannot minister from a dry vessel. We must be filled with His living water which necessitates a commitment on our part to desire and seek an increase of His presence in our lives. It also requires that we take care of ourselves by getting sufficient rest and taking time away from ministry. I will discuss that further in the following chapter.

> *Jesus answered and said to her, "If you knew the gift of God, and who it is who says to you, 'Give Me a drink,' you would have asked Him, and He would have given you living water."*
>
> (John 4:10)

Chapter Nine

Rest and Time Away

The subject of rest and time away is not something that I have seen much written or taught about. Many Christians believe that unless they continually exhaust themselves *for the Lord* they are not doing enough. However, a lack of rest is one of the quickest ways to be defeated by the devil. Whether you serve the Lord in an official position or not, resting and taking time away from your normal responsibilities is a necessity.

Nonstop busyness is one of the most frequent tactics that the enemy uses to gain victory over Christians who are serving the Lord. If the devil cannot stop us from ministering, he will send plenty of people our way to help us get burned-out. I am including this chapter because I have realized, through experience, the utmost importance of balance when you are ministering to the brokenhearted.

Jesus did not minister nonstop! Why should we believe that it is God's will for us to do so? Jesus went up to the mountain alone to pray after ministering to the multitudes as recorded in Matthew 14:23. If Jesus considered it important to rest and take time away from ministry, we should follow His example and do the same. Otherwise, our spiritual, emotional, and physical strength *will* be exhausted.

It is so easy to get out of balance in *doing* for the Lord. In the past, well-meaning believers advised us to increase our involvement in many areas of ministry including training people, scheduling more seminars, accepting additional speaking opportunities, and traveling wherever necessary to help the ministry expand. At first, this sounded good. After all, it has been said that you do not slow down when a ministry is expanding. The pressure that comes is to do more. Do more. *Do more!* That is not always the Lord's plan.

In fact, while I was spending time with the Lord in December 2010, He specifically said, *"Slow down.* Faster is *not* better. More is *not* better. Bigger is *not* better." My health was being affected significantly by all of the pressure to do more. God definitely told me to put the brakes on the pace we were trying to keep or the outcome would be disastrous. So, I obeyed Him and prayed about which areas I needed to spend my spiritual, emotional, and physical energy on and how to reduce my involvement in other areas.

Many Christians quote Philippians 4:13, "I can do all things through Christ who strengthens me." That verse does *not* mean that we are to try to be superhuman and push ourselves beyond our physical, emotional, and spiritual ability. We are not designed to continue at an ever accelerating high-speed pace. If we do, we will eventually "hit the wall." The Lord rested on the seventh day and He instructs us in His Word to rest as well. Not doing so is not just unwise but it is disobedience to God.

> *There remains therefore a rest for the people of God.*
> *For He who has entered His rest has himself also*
> *ceased from his works as God did from His. Let us*
> *therefore be diligent to enter that rest, lest anyone fall*
> *according to the same example of disobedience.*
>
> (Hebrews 4:9-11)

I am not saying that it is wrong for a ministry to increase in size. I am saying that if balance is not maintained in a person's life, the results can be devastating. We have all witnessed the downfall of high profile people in ministry as a result of the more-is-better mentality.

That mind-set can drive people past the point of wisdom. We must always remember that the world's ways are not to be our ways. The Bible instructs us in Romans 12:2, "Do not be conformed to this world, but be transformed by the renewing of your mind, that you may prove what is that good and acceptable and perfect will of God."

I have learned to ask the Lord about everything and to not do anything different unless I hear from Him. This includes taking time to rest and get away from ministry. The more intense the ministry became that we were involved in, the more we needed to schedule time to rest. This did not line up with our previous Christian training. We were taught that "time is short" and we must work harder and longer to accomplish the Lord's will on this earth. How much sense does that make if we completely burn out as a result of pushing ourselves in serving the Lord? Of course, it doesn't make any sense. That is why we must seek the Lord's will and obey His leading regardless of what others may say. Balance in ministry is found in the Lord's wisdom.

> *If any of you lacks wisdom, let him ask of God, who gives to all liberally and without reproach, and it will be given to him.*
>
> (James 1:5)

Praying with those who are spiritually and/or emotionally wounded and doing spiritual warfare on their behalf is one of the most draining ministries in which anyone can be involved. If we do not practice resting in the Lord and taking time away from ministry, we will soon find ourselves depleted and struggling to continue. This does not honor God nor does it show the world that we, as followers of Jesus, are any different from them. However, resting and taking time away from ministry is not easy. The enemy will say, "You are wasting time. You should be doing this or that. You are being lazy."

They are all lies from the devil and meant to heap nothing but guilt and condemnation on us.

The devil will also try to create "emergencies" and "urgent" situations to keep us weary and exhaust our energy. He is an expert at sending lots of people our way who "need" us to pray with them and making us feel like we cannot say no. The Lord has made it absolutely clear to me that *saying no* is essential *when He leads me to say no.*

Allowing ourselves to get into a weakened state also gives the enemy the best chance of success against us in the battle. When we are tired and depleted, we are a much easier target for the devil. Just as a wolf will go after a sheep that is less able to fight back, the enemy goes after ministers who have given all for the Body of Christ and have nothing left with which to fight him or his assistants.

Our ability to hear the Lord can also be effected by a state of weariness. Again, this is another part of the enemy's desired result in encouraging us to push ourselves or allow ourselves to be pushed to exhaustion. Not only do we become too weak to fight him, but we can become too weak to pray and ask the Lord for help. Many have given up at this point and turned from God. They have said, "It's not working." What is not working is that they are not resting as the Lord has instructed us to do. When we follow His instructions and rest, the Lord fills us again with His strength and peace, and our ability to hear Him returns or becomes even more fine-tuned.

As I said earlier, "praying with those who are spiritually and/or emotionally wounded and doing spiritual warfare on their behalf is one of the most draining ministries that anyone can be involved in." I have often felt my energy depleted after ministering either to individuals or to a group. There is a perfect example of this in Jesus' ministry in Luke 8:43-46. It is the account of the woman with the issue of blood touching the border of Jesus' garment and being healed. In verse 46, Jesus said, "Somebody touched Me, for I perceived power going out from Me." When the power of God flows through me during ministry, I can feel it in my physical body. I can also feel it spiritually and emotionally. Resting as the Lord leads enables me to get refilled and refreshed with His strength.

Another thing I have discovered in the past regarding the lack of rest was that I often did not realize how weary I had allowed myself to become. We can get used to the state of weariness! Only after getting away and slowing down for a few days did it become glaringly evident that my strength had greatly decreased. When this is the case, I feel like a different person after resting for a period of time.

Therefore, we *must* make taking time to rest a priority in our lives. I have found that I have to schedule days to rest and blocks of time to completely get away from ministry to get refreshed and strengthened. Sometimes this means leaving town but it frequently means shutting off the phone and computer to focus on the Lord and His restorative peace.

> *For thus says the Lord God, the Holy One of Israel:*
> *"In returning and rest you shall be saved; in quietness*
> *and confidence shall be your strength."*
>
> (Isaiah 30:15)

> *But those who wait on the LORD shall renew their*
> *strength; they shall mount up with wings like eagles,*
> *they shall run and not be weary, they shall walk and*
> *not faint.*
>
> (Isaiah 40:31)

Another important aspect of resting and taking time away from ministry is *playing*. Jill Austin told a wonderful story about hiring a new assistant several years ago. After interviewing the lady and telling her that she was hired, Jill showed her the stack of work that she would need to tackle. Then, Jill told the woman that they were going to leave the office and go to a movie theater. The woman was very surprised and asked about all the work that was waiting for her. Jill explained that anyone who worked with her must know how to play. If not, they would soon burn out. I have found this to be excellent advice. Nevertheless, some of us must learn how to play!

The Bible says in Nehemiah 8:10, "Do not sorrow, for the joy of the LORD is your strength." Too many Christians do not exhibit the joy of the Lord or any joy at all. They seem to be sad and joyless most of the time. This may be due to past pain and trauma that they have experienced that is suppressed below the surface. There is freedom available through inner healing ministry to all who will pursue it. We must actively go after that healing and the *joy of the Lord* in our lives!

> *A merry heart makes a cheerful countenance, but by sorrow of the heart the spirit is broken.*
>
> (Proverbs 15:13)

> *A merry heart does good, like medicine, but a broken spirit dries the bones.*
>
> (Proverbs 17:22)

Therefore, we must practice *playing* as a means of strengthening our bodies, souls, and spirits. For some people, me included, this is not an easy task. I have a tendency to be goal-oriented and have to fight the temptation to work rather than rest or play. With the Lord's help, I have made great progress in this area which has had a major role in my ability to stay in the battle for over twenty-five years. *Praise the Lord!*

It should be evident to you by now that rest and time away is not an option for those in ministry. Still, I can hear some of you saying, "But my church needs me. Brother so-and-so or sister so-and-so needs me. The ministry cannot go on without me." Seriously? I don't think so. If that is truly the case, then you should seek the Lord about how you can arrange things for you to be able to take time away from those demands and responsibilities. Many times, people will rely on ministers instead of relying on the Lord Jesus Christ. I am not saying that they do not need Jesus "with skin on," but that we should not let them continually come to us rather than going to Him. That can easily happen, and we must be aware when it does that the Lord may not want us to say yes as often.

I have learned many lessons regarding the importance of rest and time away from ministry over the years. There were many times when I did not rest as I should have, and I paid the price for not doing so. The years during which I operated the Christian bookstore for the Lord were a good example of this. As a result of the spiritual warfare being so intense, the numerous, exhausting hours needed to keep things running at a level of excellence, the prayer ministry with the customers, and the Christian concerts we sponsored, I got extremely weary at times. *By God's grace*, I made it through those years without "coming apart at the seams." It would have been much easier if I would have understood the importance of rest from ministry at the time. I am exceedingly grateful to the Lord for all He has taught me in this area, and I am still learning. I now try to be much more sensitive to the Lord's "still small voice" regarding rest.

In the fall of 2010, the Lord made it very clear that Bob and I needed to take a break (sabbatical) from many years of personal ministry. However, at the time, I could not imagine how that was ever going to come to pass. I was scheduling appointments three months in advance and had dozens of ladies who were depending on me for *Healing the Brokenhearted Ministry* sessions. When the Lord impressed on my heart that I needed to start working on arranging a sabbatical, I obeyed. I began by researching Christian sabbaticals on the Internet. There were several articles that I printed and read to learn how to do it in a way that glorified the Lord.

Bob and I prayed for the Lord's guidance and wisdom regarding the timing, ministry recipients, financial considerations, and plan for the sabbatical season. We discussed it with our Board of Directors, and when the Lord had given us the answers, we presented the entire plan to them. They unanimously encouraged us to take the break.

The answers to our questions regarding the details did not come all at once though. The first step was to stop accepting applications for ministry from new people. That began in November 2010. We had trained several ministers who were qualified and willing to receive applications from those who contacted us requesting ministry. At the time, I did not recognize how important this step would be to the fulfillment of the sabbatical plan but it was critical. As my list of new ministry recipients decreased, I was able to decrease the number of appointments on my schedule. Bob did not have the same concern since the number of men requesting ministry was less. Interestingly enough, as we approached the date for the sabbatical to begin, we began receiving applications from men at a much higher rate. I believe that this was a test. Bob obeyed the Lord and started referring men to one of the male ministers that he had trained.

In the spring of 2011, the Lord gave us the date when we would begin this sabbatical. It was July 1, 2011, approximately nine months after we first began seeking the Lord about it, and it would last three months. It was an enormous step of faith for me to think about refraining from doing personal ministry for such a significant period of time. Thankfully, the Lord had already prepared the way for this to occur although I still did not know the entire plan. The Lord gave me instructions for what He wanted me to do during this sabbatical period, and I was determined to obey Him. Those instructions included beginning the manuscript for this book.

For many years, I have known that someday I would write a book. As I've shared my testimony with people, they have said, "You need to write a book." I've always thought that it would happen eventually but as our ministry grew, the less I was able to see that it could actually become a reality. When I began praying about taking a sabbatical, the thought of writing a book was not anywhere in my mind. Amazingly, it was in God's plan!

In addition to writing this book, the Lord also told me other things that He wanted me to do during the sabbatical not the least of which was *rest and get refreshed*. A week after we started the sabbatical, Bob and I went to a Christian retreat for ministers, Eagle Mountain Lodge, located in northern New Mexico. I had found their information in one of the articles on the Internet about Christian sabbaticals. It was a wonderful place to start this book and to begin my time of getting refreshed. I also had to schedule time to rest and get away during the sabbatical since it would have been too easy for me to get wrapped up in doing other things.

Spending quality time with the Lord has always been my passion, but in the midst of a busy ministry schedule that can become increasingly difficult to accomplish. I found myself having to fight for that time far too often. During the sabbatical, I had to be diligent in taking advantage of the opportunity to rest in the Lord. I did it as much as possible listening carefully to the leading of the Holy Spirit regarding *my* plan for the day or week and changing it to line up with the Lord's plan. Obedience is the key!

Peace with God increases significantly as we obey Him and take time to rest. Many do not ask the Lord about His will for resting in Him because they do not want to have to obey. That is so sad when we think about the fact that God has the best plan for us. Much of our trouble comes from not asking Him about His will. We can know His will in general from the Bible, but to know His perfect will for each of us individually, we must have a relationship with Him in which we allow Him to rearrange our plans. We cannot let the burden of *our* plans keep us from receiving the wonderful gift of rest that Jesus offers us in Matthew 11:28-30.

> *"Come to Me, all you who labor and are heavy laden, and I will give you rest. Take My yoke upon you and learn from Me, for I am gentle and lowly in heart, and you will find rest for your souls. For My yoke is easy and My burden is light."*

Something that was on my heart about the sabbatical was my concern for the ladies to whom I had been ministering. People that have compassion for the brokenhearted, as I do, often carry a heavy burden for those with whom they pray. If that burden is not released in a godly way, it can weigh us down and have significant unwanted effects on us. So, when the Lord provided the answer regarding my ministry recipients, I was so relieved.

One of the ladies that I had trained to do *Healing the Brokenhearted Ministry*, Gaile Mitchell of *Light Choices Ministries*, offered to help me in any way necessary to facilitate the sabbatical becoming a reality. That was a huge answer to prayer! Through Gaile and other ladies that I had trained, the ministry recipients that needed ongoing sessions would be cared for. Gaile took the responsibility of arranging ministry for my precious ladies that were not yet ready to be released from the inner healing prayer process. *Praise the Lord!*

The Lord also took care of the financial considerations for the sabbatical. Since a large part of the donations to the ministry come from people who have received prayer, we needed an increase in outside donations during the sabbatical season. We never charge for ministry but have always operated on an offering basis. Therefore, no one is ever denied ministry due to a financial lack in their lives. Miraculously, the Lord led several people to give larger donations to *All for Jesus Ministries* before and during the sabbatical which offset the absence of donations from ministry recipients. God has always supplied all our need (Philippians 4:19), and this time was no exception.

The sabbatical in 2011 was an incredible testimony of God's provision for us in many ways. It also taught me much more about the crucial need for ministers to rest and take a break from ministry. The Lord loves us no matter how many hours we spend serving Him. That will never change but if we don't take time off, rest, and play, eventually we will be of no help to anyone. When others who do not understand make comments that indicate their ignorance of the issue, we have to forgive them and go on. We cannot allow the demands of people to dictate our schedules. We must go to the Lord for His guidance and be at peace because all that really matters is that we are following *His* directions. His ways are superior to our ways!

> *"For My thoughts are not your thoughts, nor are your ways My ways," says the LORD. "For as the heavens are higher than the earth, so are My ways higher than your ways, and My thoughts than your thoughts."*
> (Isaiah 55:8-9)

Not taking time to rest and get refreshed is one trap that the devil sets for Christians in general. In the next three chapters, I will discuss several other traps that the Lord has revealed to me over the years. The first one is allowing ministry to become an idol.

Idolatry boils down to disloyalty
and can be considered adultery in our hearts.

Chapter Ten

Ministry or Idolatry?

D oes this sound like a crazy question? It's not. The Lord
God does not want us to have any idols in our lives and
that includes ministry. If you are currently serving the Lord
Jesus in a ministry and have a difficult time taking time away to rest,
your ministry may be on the verge of becoming an idol to you or it
may already be one.

There are a lot of warnings in God's Word about idols and not
having them. They begin in the Ten Commandments.

> *"You shall have no other gods before Me."*
> (Exodus 20:3)

This is the first of the Ten Commandments and God told us not to
have any other gods—idols—in our lives. An idol is something that
takes the place of God in our hearts. It can be anything that we allow
to come before Him including family, pets, material possessions,
wealth, pursuits, career, and ministry. Society encourages people to
chase after the newest, biggest, fastest, latest and greatest thing, but
as followers of Jesus we are called to chase after God alone. There is
only one, true God and He is a jealous God. He will *not* bless your
ministry if you put it before your relationship with Him.

Idolatry boils down to disloyalty and can be considered adultery in our hearts. If we are in love with anyone or anything more than we love the Most High God, we are not obeying His commandment. Any time that we make decisions based on anything but His will and direction, we have put an idol in place of Him—our own will.

Jesus warned us in Matthew 6:24, "No one can serve two masters; for either he will hate the one and love the other, or else he will be loyal to the one and despise the other. You cannot serve God and mammon." Synonyms for *mammon* are wealth, money, greed, ambition, and prosperity. Putting any of these before God is idolatry, just as putting ministry before God is idolatry. Many ministers have gotten off track in this way and suffered the consequences.

> *Therefore put to death your members which are on the earth: fornication, uncleanness, passion, evil desire, and covetousness, which is idolatry.*
>
> (Colossians 3:5)

Satan is good at tempting us to put things, people, or even our ministry before the Lord. He tried it with Jesus three different ways in the wilderness. First, he tempted Jesus with food because Jesus was fasting and hungry, but Jesus resisted the devil.

> *Then Jesus was led up by the Spirit into the wilderness to be tempted by the devil. And when He had fasted forty days and forty nights, afterward He was hungry. Now when the tempter came to Him, he said, "If You are the Son of God, command that these stones become bread."*
>
> (Matthew 4:1-3)

Then, in Matthew 4:6, Satan tried to trick Jesus into testing God by misquoting the Scriptures from Psalm 91, but Jesus refused and quoted Deuteronomy 6:16 in Matthew 4:7. Testing God in this way would have been a form of idolatry because it would have put what Satan said before God's Word. We need to follow this example of Jesus and obey God's Word regardless of what anyone else may think or say.

> *Then the devil took Him up into the holy city, set Him on the pinnacle of the temple, and said to Him, "If You are the Son of God, throw Yourself down."*
>
> (Matthew 4:5-6)

> *Jesus said to him, "It is written again, 'You shall not tempt the LORD your God.'"*
>
> (Matthew 4:7)

Last, Satan offered Jesus "all the kingdoms of the world and their glory." He was playing his best hand to try and get Jesus to make something an idol and betray His Father, the Most High God. It became crystal clear that Satan's goal was to try and entice Jesus into making him god above Yahweh, the One True God. However, Jesus knew exactly what the devil was doing and He denied Satan victory over His loyalty to His Heavenly Father.

> *Again, the devil took Him up on an exceedingly high mountain, and showed Him all the kingdoms of the world and their glory. And he said to Him, "All these things I will give You if You will fall down and worship me." Then Jesus said to him, "Away with you, Satan! For it is written, 'You shall worship the LORD your God, and Him only you shall serve.'"*
>
> (Matthew 4:8-10)

We must learn to be this loyal to God in every area of our lives including, and especially, in ministry. Again, the Lord holds us accountable for what has been revealed to us. We cannot try to tell Him that we did not know, or understand a biblical principle, when *He knows* that we just made the decision to ignore it and disobey Him. God knows everything and we have to stop playing games with Him. We are responsible to live what He has told us to the best of our ability. The Lord must be *number one* in our hearts!

Some Christians have embraced the belief that if the Lord calls you into a ministry it should be number one, before everything else in your life. However, the Bible clearly states that we are to love God and love others as our first and second priorities. These are Jesus' words!

> *Jesus said to him, "'You shall love the LORD your God with all your heart, with all your soul, and with all your mind.' This is the first and great commandment. And the second is like it: 'You shall love your neighbor as yourself.'"*

(Matthew 22:37-39)

Many families of people who serve the Lord in ministry have been hurt tremendously and have even been destroyed as the result of the ministry becoming an idol! There is usually deception involved as well when this is the case because the family members have to pretend to everyone else that everything is okay. The minister and ministry may have accomplished great things for the Lord, but the minister's personal life has fallen apart due to an out-of-balance attitude toward the ministry. This does *not* honor our Most High God in any way. The Lord wants Christian ministries to succeed and be fruitful, but He is much more concerned about the fruit in our personal lives. If we neglect our relationship with Him—or our families—the ministry has become an idol.

> *For this you know, that no fornicator, unclean person, nor covetous man, who is **an idolater**, has any inheritance in the kingdom of Christ and God.*
> (Ephesians 5:5, emphasis added)

According to the verse above, idolaters will not go to heaven. There is an even stronger warning in Matthew 7 about people ministering and expecting to go to heaven who are eventually told by Jesus that they never knew Him!

> *"Not everyone who says to Me, 'Lord, Lord,' shall enter the kingdom of heaven, but he who does the will of My Father in heaven. Many will say to Me in that day, 'Lord, Lord, have we not prophesied in Your name, cast out demons in Your name, and done many wonders in Your name?' And then I will declare to them, 'I never knew you; depart from Me, you who practice lawlessness!'"*
> (Matthew 7:21-23)

This should be a huge wake-up call for those in ministry. Just because a ministry bears fruit does not mean that those involved are walking with the Lord as the Bible instructs. Our *obedience* to the Lord is vital and shows that we love Him above all else. We will *not* go to heaven just because we said a prayer *at one time*. If Jesus Christ is *truly* our *Lord*, we must obey Him! Deuteronomy 28 lists the blessings of obedience and the consequences of disobedience. Many people in ministry have suffered consequences—including the destruction of their family—due to their disobedience to the will of God. *Putting ministry first is disobedience to the will of God.*

In Luke 10:38-42, Jesus made it very clear that serving should not take priority over sitting at His feet. Martha was very busy with preparations to serve the Lord and even allowed herself to get irritated at Mary because she was not helping her. However, Jesus said, "Mary has chosen that good part." Serving the Lord is an amazing privilege, but it should *never* take priority over spending time with Him.

Your obedience to the Lord in every area of your life is your responsibility. Allowing ministry to become number one in your heart above everything else, including the Lord and your family, is a definite trap set by the kingdom of darkness.

> *"and you have persevered and have patience, and have labored for My name's sake and have not become weary. Nevertheless I have this against you, that you have left your first love."*
>
> (Revelation 2:3-4)

If this describes you, do whatever it takes to return to your first love—Jesus!

Chapter Eleven

Other Traps

W hen we begin to serve God, the devil enlarges the bull's-eye on us. His plans to deter us from our calling are no different now than they were thousands of years ago. The Lord has allowed me to learn and grow in numerous ways in ministry, and the enemy has also increased and changed the nature of his attacks as I have become better at identifying his schemes. It is warfare, and just as warfare in the physical realm changes depending on the effectiveness of the outcome, so does the nature of the Adversary's attacks change in spiritual warfare against us. Once a form of attack or trap does not work for him, he will switch to another method. A trap can only be successful if we walk into it. I will discuss some additional traps that the devil sets for us in this chapter.

Complacency and apathy about spiritual warfare is one tactic the devil uses to prevent Christians from being as effective and as productive as they could be for the Lord. Thinking that the devil and his associates have no power over us, because somehow we are protected from him because we have accepted Jesus Christ as our Lord and Savior, has gotten many believers in serious trouble. The Bible warns us about the devil's ability to harm us and take us down the road of destruction. We must not be complacent or apathetic regarding his plans. If the blood of Jesus protected us from all of the effects of the battle with the kingdom of darkness, the passages in the

Word about spiritual warfare would be needless. Since they are there, we should take them as a vital warning from the Lord.

Not recognizing the works of darkness or denying that something is an attack from the enemy are also huge traps. We must learn to recognize the works of the kingdom of darkness and be diligent in reacting appropriately to them and in resisting them. Ignorance about what the enemy is trying to do to stop us in our tracks is one of the traps that he sets for us. This is why, I believe, that we are admonished by Jesus in Matthew 10:16 to be "wise as serpents."

"Behold, I send you out as sheep in the midst of wolves. Therefore be wise as serpents and harmless as doves."

We must learn how to spot the devil's signature in our lives. Learn about his tactics and then apply the appropriate response for that scheme. Many people have "book knowledge" but have not put what they have learned into practice on a daily basis. That does not work. It does not matter how much you know unless you apply it in your life!

However, it is not wise to call everything an attack from the enemy either. I have witnessed believers who have gone overboard in this area and given the devil and his forces much more credit than they deserve. There are natural consequences in our lives for our actions and sometimes what a person calls an attack from the enemy is just the consequence of their own behavior. If you spend money in an irresponsible way and end up bankrupt, the consequence is a result of your actions. Our free will is often the cause of misery in our lives. The devil can tempt us to do ungodly and sinful things, but he cannot force us to do them.

We need to call *sin* what it is and stop blaming the devil for the results of our sin. As followers of Jesus, we have an enormous responsibility to hate sin and do our utmost to avoid it. The devil is a legalist, and he will use every chance we give him to retaliate against us. Known sin in our lives is a wide-open door for the kingdom of darkness. Therefore, as I have already said, as the Lord reveals an area of sin in our lives, we must ask Him for forgiveness and turn from that sin. The Bible contains abundant instructions about repentance or turning from sin. In order to repent, we must change the way we think to line up with God's perspective. Walking in known sin and not repenting is a serious trap that we must become diligent to avoid!

As I discussed in chapter nine, weariness and fatigue are extremely common traps that Satan sets for believers. There is a remedy for these traps. Obeying the Lord and resting from the work of the ministry and from all other work will prevent this scheme from being successful. Resting from ministry but continuing to work on other things in place of ministry is not a wise solution to accomplish the restoration needed for our bodies. We must rest from all endeavors that drain our physical, emotional, and spiritual energy. I cannot stress this enough! Weariness will result in nothing but negative outcomes. Resting and taking time away from the normal demands of life are the only antidote to this maneuver from the Adversary.

There are godly answers to the other traps that the enemy sets for believers as well. Scripture says in 1 Corinthians 10:13, "No temptation has overtaken you except such as is common to man; but God is faithful, who will not allow you to be tempted beyond what you are able, but with the temptation will also make the way of escape, that you may be able to bear it."

Not setting godly boundaries in our own lives is a temptation and a trap that the devil uses repeatedly, especially with ministers. Most ministers are compassionate. That is why they have entered ministry. They desire to help people and this desire drives them at times to neglect the wisdom of the Lord in setting healthy, godly boundaries in their lives. I have been guilty of this in the past.

When we opened the Christian bookstore in 1991, all I wanted to do was serve the Lord and the people that He sent to me. Too often, I worked too many hours, and I frequently said, "Yes," when I should have said, "No." I can see this now but at the time I thought that I was being a good servant. I would regularly come home so exhausted that I could do nothing other than lay down on the couch. I did not even have the energy to eat dinner.

During the time when the store was attached to our home, I would open early or stay open late for someone to accommodate their "needs" even though they were not emergency situations. My boundaries were out of line and almost nonexistent. As the years passed, I became increasingly weary, not just due to a lack of rest and time away, but also as a result of not setting godly boundaries. By God's grace and mercy, I have learned from those mistakes.

Connected to the practice of not having healthy boundaries is the trap of the fear of man. This is another very successful strategy of the kingdom of darkness. The fear of man and what a person may think or do if we do not make them happy and comply with their requests or demands was one of the most difficult things for me to overcome. Growing up, I learned that the fear of man, especially fear of my father, would often keep me out of trouble. Then that belief was reinforced in my marriage to my first husband. The fear of man became stronger as I got older. I would do anything to please people to avoid the consequences of not doing so.

After I became a Christian, the Lord began working on this ungodly pattern in my life, and I slowly became progressively freer from the fear of man. During a Christian conference I was attending in 2006, I heard the Lord say, "Let the fear of man go." At that time, I thought that I had already done so, but in the weeks after the conference the Lord showed me areas where I was still bound by that fear. I needed a new level of freedom from that trap of the enemy, and the Lord prepared me for what was coming that could have ensnared me once again. I have since realized that freedom from the fear of man is something that happens in levels and usually over a long period of time. We are only responsible to the Lord to change what

He reveals to us and to obey Him to accomplish that change. As we do, another trap of the enemy is thwarted!

Unrealistic expectations of ourselves are tied to the fear of man. If we expect that we can please everyone, we are sadly mistaken. The only One who we should be consistent in pleasing is God. A reverent fear of Him should override any fear of man. God does not have unrealistic expectations of us. He knows us better than we know ourselves, and we should only desire His will in our lives. He has told us in His Word that His peace comes as we obey Him.

> *Finally, brethren, whatever things are true, whatever things are noble, whatever things are just, whatever things are pure, whatever things are lovely, whatever things are of good report, if there is any virtue and if there is anything praiseworthy—meditate on these things. The things which you learned and received and heard and saw in me, these do, and the God of peace will be with you.*
>
> (Philippians 4:8-9)

> *Behold, to obey is better than sacrifice,*
>
> (1 Samuel 15:22)

One specific unrealistic expectation that the enemy quite often attempts to use against those in ministry is that we should be able to help everyone. Thinking that every person to whom we minister will receive at the same level is just not true. I had a very real encounter with this trap when Bob and I began doing *Healing the Brokenhearted Ministry* prayer sessions.

One person who was wounded emotionally in the past asked us to pray with them. They were *desperate* for freedom. Many others had tried to help this person get free from the torment they were living with. However, when we prayed with this person, it was like ministering to a brick wall. We explained the ministry in the same way we had done with numerous other people. The Holy Spirit gave us several different avenues to explore and we exhausted everything we knew to do in order to help this afflicted Christian. In the end, the person stated that they *did not believe* that a broken heart was their problem. This person had been divorced, had lost custody of their children, had been fired from their job, and had been given many negative labels. Every one of those experiences would cause a person's heart to be broken. Nevertheless, they were not in agreement with our evaluation of their situation.

I talked to the Lord a lot that night and the next day asking Him what we did wrong that we were unable to help that person. I searched and searched for the answer to the blockage in their freedom. I read excerpts from different books looking for what we had missed. Then, I heard the Lord clearly say, "People will only receive what they believe." *That was it!* The Lord set me free from the unrealistic expectation that everyone would be helped by the ministry that we offered. It sounds like a simple reality but when your heart is to help people, you can get caught up in that trap. The person described above did not accept the fact that Jesus, through our prayer ministry, could help them, and that blocked the ministry from being successful.

So, let go of any unrealistic expectations that you have for yourself or your ministry. This trap can lead to disappointment, guilt, condemnation, and even anger at God. Freedom from those ungodly expectations will make that trap fruitless in your life. *Praise the Lord!*

Not knowing the limit to our authority can also be an enormous trap of the devil. There are definite limits to our authority in the spiritual realm just as there are in the natural realm. Number one, God never overrules a person's free will. We cannot and should not even try to do that. The people to whom we minister need to willingly be in agreement with the ministry or it will be a waste of our time and can even be damaging to them. Several times, a parent has encouraged their son or daughter to receive ministry only to have the results of the session be less than successful. The child or teen did not want to come in the first place and they did not fully cooperate with the ministry. The same thing has happened when one spouse recommends that the other come for prayer. If a person is not seeking the ministry because *they* believe they need it, it will not be effective and no amount of authority on our part will override their free will. This trap can, again, lead to disappointment and discouragement for the minister and the ministry recipient.

Another area in which not knowing *the limit to our authority* that has often gotten Christians in major trouble is when they try to come against principalities in the spiritual realm. I discussed this regarding spiritual warfare in chapter seven. We have witnessed the results of this practice by unaware believers and it has not been good. None of us, in our right mind, would go to another country and demand that the king or queen be removed from power because we said it in Jesus' name. We would be taken away and locked up for doing such a thing. It is the same thing with the principality realm.

Since the Lord God, the Creator of the Universe, has not chosen to stop these evil entities from operating and destroyed them, who are we to think that we have the power to do so? We do not have the authority to come against principalities. Their power has been increased as a result of the allegiance of multiplied millions of people on this earth. However, there is a correct, biblically based protocol for praying regarding principalities. We do have the authority to ask God to deal with them but we do *not* have the authority to come against them directly. Again, not knowing the limits to our authority in this area can be a devastating trap. If we try to overstep our authority, we can invite retaliation from the kingdom of darkness. Remember, the Lord instructed us to be wise!

Disunity is another trap set by the devil that will always result in destruction if not dealt with according to the Lord's directions. The phrase *with one accord* is used many times in the Bible. There is a remarkable amount of power in unity. Husbands and wives are often the target of attacks from the devil because he knows the powerful results of unity between them. Unity is essential in ministry. Disunity can cause, and many times has caused, the complete collapse of a ministry.

> *I, therefore, the prisoner of the Lord, beseech you to walk worthy of the calling with which you were called, with all lowliness and gentleness, with longsuffering, bearing with one another in love, **endeavoring to keep the unity of the Spirit** in the bond of peace.*
>
> (Ephesians 4:1-3, emphasis added)

When the enemy begins to plant his seed of disunity, it must be stopped immediately. However, we must also be careful not to call every suggestion or comment that we do not agree with *disunity* or *rebellion*. Prayerfully seeking the Lord's wisdom regarding all circumstances that arise and requesting counsel from godly people who know how to keep things to themselves is crucial to avoid overreacting to a situation.

> *Where there is no counsel, the people fall; but in the multitude of counselors there is safety.*
>
> (Proverbs 11:14)

Once we have been freed from the fear of man, we can deal with disunity in a godly way and without guilt or condemnation. Remembering that obeying the Lord is our number one priority makes this much easier. Unfortunately, the Body of Christ has been subjected to this scheme of the Adversary—disunity—for a long time. It was even an issue in the early church.

Then after some days Paul said to Barnabas, "Let us now go back and visit our brethren in every city where we have preached the word of the Lord, and see how they are doing." Now Barnabas was determined to take with them John called Mark. But Paul insisted that they should not take with them the one who had departed from them in Pamphylia, and had not gone with them to the work. Then the contention became so sharp that they parted from one another. And so Barnabas took Mark and sailed to Cyprus; but Paul chose Silas and departed, being commended by the brethren to the grace of God.

(Acts 15:36-40)

Even though the Lord can turn what the enemy means for evil around for His good, if there is any way for us to resolve the disunity, we must try to the best of our ability to do so. Hearing the Lord clearly about such matters is essential. Also, it is important to give the Lord the time necessary to resolve an issue and not become impatient thereby getting ahead of God.

Impatience is another tactic that the devil uses to ensnare Christians, including those in ministry. When we pray with a person, we can become impatient and try to "help" the Lord. We must remember that His timing is always perfect, and He knows how much time a person needs for their healing to be accomplished in the best way. Discerning between interference from the enemy, interference from the person's free will, and the Lord saying *wait*, takes experience and hearing the Holy Spirit as you minister to someone. When God says *wait*, He always has a good reason. He knows so much more than we do. We must trust Him completely.

"When, God, when?" is a question that many Christians have asked over the centuries. Praying with those who have been emotionally, physically, and/or spiritually wounded and abused takes a lot of patience. Several years ago, I prayed with one lady who was going through some serious emotional abuse, and after the second prayer session, I had not seen any freedom for this dear woman. I was beginning to get impatient but the Lord told me not to give up. During the third session, the woman experienced a miraculous breakthrough. *Praise the Lord!* Don't let Satan steal freedom from anyone due to his trap of impatience.

Impatience also indicates a lack of trust in the Lord and may be due to fear of the future. These are both devices that the enemy uses to knock us off balance. The fear of the future can cause us to try to take things into our own hands instead of waiting patiently for the Lord's perfect timing. Pushing doors open *never* works. However, the Lord will not override our free will. We may get results but they are usually not the perfect plan that the Lord had in store for us if we had waited on Him. Fear of the future can also prevent us from obeying the Lord. If we fear what may happen, we may decide to take a different path. *The only safe path is in the center of God's will.* He told us in Jeremiah that His plan for us is for peace and hope.

> *For I know the thoughts that I think toward you, says the LORD, thoughts of peace and not of evil, to give you a future and a hope.*
>
> (Jeremiah 29:11)

The *fear of the future* and *not trusting God* are linked and devious traps that the devil lays for believers. Satan planted mistrust and unbelief in a human mind as far back as the Garden of Eden when, in Genesis 3:1, he asked Eve, "Has God indeed said, 'You shall not eat of every tree of the garden'?" Of course, we know the rest of the story. That seed of doubt and not trusting God led to Adam and Eve's fall. Not trusting God will always lead to destruction in our lives. We certainly cannot trust the devil. He is the father of lies. Unless we trust God, our lives, relationships, and ministries will suffer. Trusting the Lord is an absolute necessity and brings abundant blessings with it.

Be aware that the Adversary's plans and traps are meant to rob you of God's best for your life. The blessings of the Lord are worth staying in the battle. *Trusting God* is a doorway to receiving His blessings!

Trusting God becomes much easier as we receive healing and freedom from past emotional, physical, and spiritual abuse and trauma.

Chapter Twelve

Trusting God

Trusting God? You may ask how trusting God relates to healing hearts. Trusting God is essential in any believer's life but especially crucial if you are called to minister to the brokenhearted. It is also not an easy thing to do for someone who has been hurt or traumatized in the past by people, especially by other Christians. Those hurts and wounds often cause a person to blame God for what *His people* have done to them. However, God is not the author of pain in our lives. He is the One we need to turn to when things fall apart. Many times, people run from God instead. This is so destructive and playing right into the enemy's plans for us.

> *The LORD is good, a stronghold in the day of trouble;*
> *and He knows those who trust in Him.*
>
> (Nahum 1:7)

> *God is our refuge and strength, a very present help*
> *in trouble.*
>
> (Psalm 46:1)

Life is not a "bowl of cherries." No one escapes hurts and painful experiences in this life. There are so many opportunities for us to trust God, but many Christians have been led to believe that once we give our lives to the Lord everything will be a piece of cake. When that does not happen, they sometimes turn *from* the Lord. The pain and trauma does not go away but the effects stay inside the person, festering and waiting to explode like a volcano. Trusting God becomes much easier as we receive healing and freedom from past emotional, physical, and spiritual abuse and trauma. As our hearts are healed and become whole, we are able to trust the Lord in deeper levels. As we trust Him to a greater extent, He will comfort us and lead and guide us through the painful circumstances that come our way. Then, the devil has less to use against us. *Praise the Lord!*

> *I would have lost heart, unless I had believed that I would see the goodness of the LORD in the land of the living. Wait on the LORD; be of good courage, and He shall strengthen your heart; wait, I say, on the LORD!*
> (Psalm 27:13-14)

Many people, Christians included, use the excuse that bad things happened when they trusted the Lord to protect them, and therefore, they can no longer trust Him. They are playing right into the Adversary's hands. Believing that God allowed their pain and trauma because He did not care about them is just what the devil wants them to think. Then bitterness and unforgiveness toward God can take root and grow in their heart while the level of trust in God steadily decreases. This is how people can become hard-hearted and turn from God in spite of having known the truth at one time.

Trusting God is not an option if we desire peace in our lives. Regardless of what the devil brings across our path, we can have peace in the midst of the storm if we will decide to trust God. Trusting the Creator of the Universe in *every* circumstance is a vital weapon of our warfare as followers of Jesus Christ.

*For the weapons of our warfare are not carnal but mighty in God for pulling down strongholds, casting down arguments and every high thing that exalts itself **against the knowledge of God**,*

(2 Corinthians 10:4-5, emphasis added)

Trusting the Lord is essential in times of spiritual warfare. It is a life saver when the attacks come from the Adversary and his assistants. The enemy knows how much we trust the Lord by our reaction to his attacks. If we react in fear, we are not trusting that the Lord, and *not* the devil, is in charge. God never abdicates His authority to the enemy. *Never!* However, due to the sinful nature of man and man's free will, the devil has the legal right to bring certain things into our lives. Satan is a legalist. If he is given any opportunity, he will run with it.

We must learn to trust the Lord and stop putting so much trust in the devil. When given bad reports by the doctor, many will put more trust in *that* report than in the Word of God. God is able to heal regardless of what the doctor or report may say. Many times, due to a lack of experiential knowledge of God in addition to not knowing His Word, fear is allowed to come in and rule when the enemy sends adversity our way. *Fear* is trusting the devil. Faith is trusting God. We can only trust God if we know Him!

Knowing God is crucial to being able to trust Him. You cannot trust someone that you do not know. The only way to get to know the Lord is by spending time with Him. You learn about your earthly friends and your spouse because you spend time with them. That is the only way to begin to know the Lord. We will never understand or know everything about the Lord on this earth, and I am not suggesting that this is possible. He is too magnificent for our minds to completely comprehend His greatness. We can only learn to trust Him by spending quality time with Him.

*Jesus answered and said to them, "You are mistaken,
not knowing the Scriptures nor the power of God."*
(Matthew 22:29)

Reading God's Word gives us critical insight into His character. The more we understand about the Lord's character, the less we can be deceived by the devil or his workers. Recognizing the truth from a lie becomes much easier when we know the character of God. I have personally had many opportunities to discern the truth of the character of God from what the enemy tried to deceive me into believing about a circumstance. This knowledge of God's character allowed me to trust Him even when the natural situations seemed impossible.

When we were given the opportunity to move our Christian bookstore into the shopping center and water was pouring from the ceiling, down the walls, and into puddles on the floor, I knew that the Lord would not have led Mark to offer us that space if God did not have a plan to resolve the water problem. I said, "Noah had more water than that to deal with and God made a way for Noah and his family to be saved from it. The Lord is the same and will provide a solution for this water problem as well." I discussed the rest of this testimony in chapter two. The Lord took care of the problem in a way that was not expected by anyone. If I had not known about Noah and the very significant water issue that the Lord had delivered him from, my ability to trust God in this situation may not have been so strong. Knowing God's character by knowing the Scriptures increases our level of trust in Him.

When my mother and sister's house burned to the ground as we were preparing to serve the Lord in Texas, I could have blamed God for "allowing" that to happen and walked away from our calling to serve Him. However, I knew that God loved them and did not cause that fire. For some reason that we may never understand, He did not prevent it but He also protected my mom, sister, niece, and nephew from being injured or killed. *That was huge.* My mom usually returned home after taking my niece and nephew to school, and she could easily have been killed in the fire. That day, she stopped at a restaurant and ate breakfast alone which was extremely unusual for her. I know that the Lord led her to the restaurant to keep her away from the house. That morning, God answered my many prayers to keep my family safe. *Praise the Lord!*

The Scriptures also tell us in Proverbs 3:5-6, "Trust in the LORD with all your heart, and lean not on your own understanding; in all your ways acknowledge Him, and He shall direct your paths." These verses give us the answer for every situation. *We must trust the Lord with all our heart.* When a person has suffered the pain of divorce, loss of a loved one, abuse of any kind, natural disasters, and other traumatic events, their heart becomes torn apart and doing anything, let alone trusting the Lord, with *all their heart* becomes difficult. This is the main reason that people, especially Christians, should diligently seek healing for their hearts. God sent Jesus so that the brokenhearted can be set free and healed. We must do our part and cooperate with the work of the Holy Spirit to see that healing comes to pass. Trusting the Lord to begin your journey of healing is the first step to your freedom.

It is also crucial to trust the Lord if you are called to minister to the brokenhearted. During ministry sessions, we not only need to hear the Lord's voice clearly but we must trust that He knows the person to whom we are ministering better than we know them, and even better than they know themselves. Knowing the character of God allows us to discern in those times between the voice of God, our own thoughts, and the voice of the enemy. There have been numerous times when the Lord led me down a path while I was praying with someone that I had no intention of pursuing, but it became evident that the Lord had a marvelous plan for that person's session. Letting go of all preconceived ideas or plans as you minister or receive ministry is absolutely imperative. One cannot do that without trusting the Lord implicitly!

Trusting the Lord is a prerequisite to submitting to Him. We cannot fully submit to His plans and His will if we do not trust Him. Submitting to God will often require us to step out of our comfort zone which also requires a high level of trust in the Lord. What He directs us to do may go totally against the world's ideas and usually does. We must be so sold out to God that no matter what He asks us to do—which will always be in agreement with the Bible—we are willing to obey Him.

If our own hearts are not healed from past pain and trauma to the extent that we can trust the Lord at that level, we will not be as effective for the Lord in seeing the brokenhearted healed and set free. *There is no substitute for healing and freedom.* We cannot suffer our way out of the pain, deny it exists, or speak enough positive words to receive the healing that is available through Jesus Christ and Christian inner healing ministry. Memorizing Scripture about healing is wonderful and necessary in order for us to know the character and promises of God. Still, additional prayer may be needed for deep emotional and spiritual healing to occur.

The Lord can and has instantly healed many people physically, emotionally, and spiritually. Those who have not received their freedom instantly should not be condemned or made to feel like they have done something wrong that is preventing them from receiving their healing. This only piles guilt onto already hurting individuals. My experience has been that receiving inner healing prayer with a trained prayer minister is often necessary for a person to realize that they can be set free from the torment of past trauma. Many people, especially those that were molested, do not accept that what happened was *not* their fault, and it does not matter how many people have told them that truth. That belief can keep them in bondage. Jesus can release them from this through Christian inner healing prayer and He can help their eyes to be opened to the truth.

And Elisha prayed, and said, "LORD, I pray, open his eyes that he may see." Then the LORD opened the eyes of the young man, and he saw. And behold, the mountain was full of horses and chariots of fire all around Elisha.

(2 Kings 6:17)

Behold, You desire truth in the inward parts, and in the hidden part You will make me to know wisdom.

(Psalm 51:6)

The more we trust the Lord, the easier it is to look inside at the things that need healing and the greater the freedom we can receive through Jesus and His finished work on the cross. *There is nothing that God desires more for us than freedom.* That is why He sent Jesus to this earth. His sacrifice provided for our healing in every area, but we must receive and appropriate all that the Lord has made available to us and trust Him to be with us on the journey. We cannot receive everything that the Lord wants to give us if we do not trust that He will only give us good things. Sometimes the inner healing process is painful as we deal with things that we have stuffed for years or decades, but the end result is always worth the price. Just as the physical healing process may include a time of pain before the healing is complete, yet we go through it trusting that the end result will be better than the original condition, inner healing always requires us to trust that the Lord can and will set us free.

Of course, **the first step in trusting God is accepting His incomparable gift of salvation through His Son, Jesus Christ**. To ask Jesus Christ to be your Lord and Savior is freedom that cannot be found any other way. It is freedom from an eternity in hell separated from God the Father, the Creator of the Universe. The Bible says in Romans 3:23, "All have sinned and fall short of the glory of God." If we are completely honest, we will admit that we are sinners. We really don't need the Bible to confirm that truth but it is there for those who may not want to admit it. Thankfully, God did not leave us in our sinful state without a way out. Romans 5:8 says, "But God demonstrates His own love toward us, in that while we were still sinners, Christ died for us." What a tremendous gift! Jesus died, rose from the dead, and ascended into heaven so that you and I can spend eternity with Him in heaven. You must trust God enough to *receive* His incomparable gift.

If you have not taken the step of trusting the Lord with your eternity, I would encourage you to do it now. None of us know when we may take our last breath or if we will even have a second to make things right with God. In Romans 10:9, the Bible says, "If you confess with your mouth the Lord Jesus and believe in your heart that God has raised Him from the dead, you will be saved." If you *sincerely* ask Jesus to be your Lord and Savior, He will be. He loves you! Ask God to forgive you for your sins in the name of His Son, Jesus Christ, and He will. Ask the Holy Spirit to come and help you trust God for the next part of your journey. The angels in heaven rejoice when one person turns to God. It is the main and most important step toward trusting the Lord. If you have just done this, I want to be the first to welcome you to the family of God!

The next step is to acquire a Bible, and read it to get to know God. Begin in the Gospel of John and continue through the New Testament. Ask the Lord to show you in His Word what you need to know to grow in godly ways. Ask Him also to lead you to other Christians who can help you grow spiritually. You will be amazed at how quickly He will answer those prayers!

If you have previously taken that step of faith but have not been living for the Lord and need to ask Him to restore your relationship with Him, do it now. Trust Him enough to ask Him for forgiveness in Jesus' name, and then, allow the Holy Spirit to connect you with people who can help you heal from the circumstances in life that caused you to doubt the Lord. It has been my experience that anyone who walks away from the Lord did so as the result of painful and traumatic experiences. Jesus wants to heal your heart. He is the Master of healing hearts! Come back to Him. Jesus is waiting with His arms open wide. His love for you is endless, and your spiritual growth is His desire.

Our spiritual growth is often blocked by unhealed emotional and spiritual wounds.

Chapter Thirteen

Spiritual Growth

W hen we accept Jesus Christ as our personal Lord and Savior, the journey of our spiritual growth begins. For some of you, that just happened and for others, like me, you have been on your journey with the Lord for several decades. The Bible gives us a description of the wonderful path and direction for growing spiritually in the things of God in 2 Peter, chapter one.

> *add to your faith virtue, to virtue knowledge, to knowledge self-control, to self-control perseverance, to perseverance godliness, to godliness brotherly kindness, and to brotherly kindness love. For if these things are yours and abound, you will be neither barren nor unfruitful in the knowledge of our Lord Jesus Christ.*
>
> (2 Peter 1:5-8)

The Holy Spirit gives us strength and guides us along this path. However, our spiritual growth is often blocked by unhealed emotional and spiritual wounds. Most of us have been unaware of the effect that the painful and traumatic events in our lives have had on us and our ability to grow in the Lord. We all know someone who seems stuck at a certain age and who can't mature beyond that period in their life.

They, most likely, experienced some kind of emotional, physical, and/ or spiritual trauma at that age. Unless healing occurs for the pain that has been stuffed, we may struggle for years and sometimes our entire life in our walk with God.

Spiritual maturity is a process. It is not something that occurs automatically the moment after we ask Jesus into our lives. Oh, if it were just that simple! In James 1:4, we are instructed to become mature and complete, not lacking anything. This reference is one of many portions of Scripture that emphasize our responsibility to work on our spiritual growth. It is something that we, as Christians, must work on our whole lives. We must pursue spiritual maturity.

I do not believe that any of us ever reach complete spiritual maturity as long as we are on this earth. A few of my ministry recipients have asked me if I was "completely healed and whole." My answer has always been the same, "No." I am in exceedingly better shape than I was before I received any inner healing, but the Lord continues to reveal areas in my own heart that He wants to heal. I am always open to His ongoing work of healing. We receive freedom in levels. I praise God that He knows the perfect time for each of us to go through emotional and spiritual surgery for our past wounds. He is awesome! The day will come though, when we enter heaven, when everything in us will be transformed to perfection and all of our spiritual immaturity will vanish in an instant. *Praise the Lord!*

In the same way as we mature physically over a period of time, we also mature spiritually over time. There are things that we must do to assist in the process of our physical growth such as eat, exercise and sleep. Similarly, the Lord has a specific path or journey of healing, freedom, and spiritual maturing for each one of us. However, we must choose to mature spiritually and participate in the process.

A lot of guilt and self-condemnation could be avoided in the Body of Christ if our brothers- and sisters-in-the-Lord understood that much of our sin is pain driven. As long as the pain is there, we can struggle seemingly endlessly with the same patterns of sin, accumulating huge burdens of guilt along the way. That is not God's best for us. He provided the way for us to be set free from pain. We must be willing to face the things that have kept us in bondage for years and allow our Merciful and Gracious Heavenly Father to release that pain from our hearts. It is not easy but *it is worth it*!

Part of the process of spiritual growth includes *allowing* the Lord Jesus to heal our hearts. This is much easier said than done and rarely happens without the assistance of other Christians. This also requires us to get past the fear of what may happen during the healing ministry. For many Christians, this fear is very understandable.

I have personally prayed with several believers who have gone through horrible experiences trying to get free from things that have bound them for years. In the process, they were unintentionally wounded emotionally and/or spiritually, and sometimes abused, by God's people. That is why it is so important to seek out loving, trained, Christian prayer ministers and ask for referrals from friends and family. Be careful. The enemy can use our brothers- and sisters-in-the-Lord, without them even realizing it, to cause even more pain in our hearts and spirits. If that describes you, I would encourage you to ask the Lord to give you the strength you need to pursue the healing that Jesus died to provide for you.

Fear not, for I am with you; be not dismayed, for I am your God. I will strengthen you, yes, I will help you, I will uphold you with My righteous right hand.
(Isaiah 41:10)

For God has not given us a spirit of fear, but of power and of love and of a sound mind.
(2 Timothy 1:7)

Ungodly fear can also be attached to the pain that we have so necessarily suppressed in order to continue to function in our daily lives. Once that pain is released to Jesus, the ungodly fear no longer has a legal right to stay. The devil knows this and he does all he can to keep believers from learning the truth. Jesus wants us to know the truth!

> *"And you shall know the truth, and the truth shall make you free."*
>
> (John 8:32)

If you have suffered any kind of spiritual hurt or abuse by other Christians, you also have the opportunity to practice forgiveness toward whoever was responsible for your pain. That may be difficult because you may have told yourself that *they know God* and should not have done those things to you. Nevertheless, Christians can often be the hardest on each other.

We must face the reality that holding unforgiveness is counterproductive in our own lives. Again, forgiving them is not—in any way—saying that what they did was right, but it will release you from the effects that unforgiveness has on you. It is for *your* benefit to forgive them not theirs. God will deal with them. You are responsible for you. If the pain is too overwhelming for you to forgive them, seek help to get free from the pain. Don't let it destroy you!

One of the ladies that I have prayed with extensively was repeatedly hurt and abused spiritually by other Christians. When she came to me for *Healing the Brokenhearted Ministry*, the amount of emotional and spiritual pain she was carrying was overwhelming. She had forgiven most of those who had caused the pain to the best of her ability. Still, the pain was hidden in deep places in her heart and she did not know how to release it to Jesus. She did not even know how much of it was hidden. Many tears were shed during her sessions, but they were cleansing tears that led to new levels of freedom for her each time. It was not an instant freedom that she received, but a slow process of loving and compassionate prayer that helped her get set free from years of spiritual abuse.

In Luke 4, Jesus quoted Isaiah 61 saying that the Scripture was fulfilled in Him.

> *And He was handed the book of the prophet Isaiah. And when He had opened the book, He found the place where it was written:*
>
> > *"The Spirit of the LORD is upon Me, because He has anointed Me to preach the gospel to the poor; **He has sent Me to heal the brokenhearted**, to proclaim liberty to the captives and recovery of sight to the blind, to set at liberty those who are oppressed; to proclaim the acceptable year of the LORD."*
>
> *Then He closed the book, and gave it back to the attendant and sat down. And the eyes of all who were in the synagogue were fixed on Him. And He began to say to them, "Today this Scripture is fulfilled in your hearing."*
>
> (Luke 4:17-21, emphasis added)

Jesus came to heal the brokenhearted and set the captives free. I have seen hundreds of examples in my years of prayer ministry that Jesus can and does *heal the brokenhearted*. The lady that had been so spiritually abused by other believers was definitely brokenhearted but Jesus has been faithful to set her free from an enormous amount of emotional pain and trauma. Her healing journey has been a beautiful thing and a privilege to witness. Helping to facilitate it has been an enormous blessing for me. I *thank God* for His wonderful gift of healing broken hearts through Jesus!

However, I want to stress the fact that we have to be willing participants in the process of inner healing. Just as we have to be ready and willing to accept Jesus Christ as our Lord and Savior, we have to be ready and willing to receive inner healing. The Lord will allow us to *go around the mountain* one more time if we choose to do so. He will not force anyone to receive any of the gifts that He has for them. Many people have no understanding of the love and freedom that is available to them. *This is so sad.* Many do not comprehend how their spiritual growth has been stunted and how much they are missing in their relationship with Jesus, the Lover of our souls.

As we make the choice to pursue spiritual growth, obedience to the Lord is essential. The more we obey Him, the more quickly we will mature. We have a sandblasted sign hanging on the wall in our home that says, "When God tells you to do something, don't ask for a second opinion." I have heard Christians say that they do not ask for a second opinion when God tells them to do something. However, they do not realize that when they say *no* to God, they are putting their own opinion above God's opinion.

Hearing the Lord and deciding to *pray about* doing what He is telling us to do is no different. *Delay is disobedience!* Obedience is not optional if we want to grow in the Lord. Also, obedience with the right heart attitude is *submission* to God. Just obeying out of obligation or knowledge is not what God desires either. The Lord knows our hearts! He is not fooled by an act of obedience when in our heart, we are resentful of what He has told us to do. Our motives must be godly for our obedience to be true submission to God's will. I have observed Christians who do something for the Lord "in obedience" only to gain some desired result from the action. That is playing games with God.

Spiritual growth will only be achieved as we pursue holiness out of our love for God. That love increases as we mature in Him and our understanding of His incredible love and mercy for us expands.

We will *never* grasp the depth of His love for us completely, but He allows us to continue to learn about it all the days of our lives.

Sometimes the school of "hard knocks" is a better teacher than anything on our journey of spiritual growth. Going through the storms of life helps us to mature if we let the Lord teach us what we need to learn in those times. Fighting adversity is not always the answer. Sometimes, the Lord permits the trial to bring about another level of spiritual growth in us. We have to increase in our discernment to know the difference between an outright attack from the kingdom of darkness and an opportunity from the Lord. There are times when God opposes us more than the devil.

Experience is a priceless and essential ingredient in spiritual growth. You cannot bypass the knowledge and wisdom gained through years of experiencing both the Lord's hand giving you a chance to grow in Him and the tactics of the Adversary to hinder your growth. The Lord uses both to take us to new levels of maturity!

> *Behold, I have refined you, but not as silver; I have tested you in the furnace of affliction.*
>
> (Isaiah 48:10)

Some ask, "How can a loving God *allow* His children to go through difficult and sometimes destructive situations?" Parents can understand this. We can tell a child not to do something dozens of times and, once in a while, they will listen to us. Often though, children need to experience the consequences of their choices for them to learn and grow in an area. We, as God's children, frequently have to learn the same way. Remembering that He is the Master Potter and we are the clay helps immensely as we travel the path of spiritual growth.

> *But now, O LORD, You are our Father; we are the*
> *clay, and You our potter; and all we are the work of*
> *Your hand.*
>
> (Isaiah 64:8)

The Master Potter has done a lot of work on this piece of clay over the past twenty-seven years. I am very thankful for all the circumstances that He used to contribute to who I am at this point in my life. Even though some of them were excruciatingly painful, I value the lessons I learned from each situation. I cannot share many of the most painful experiences that I have gone through because doing so would involve divulging information that would in turn hurt other people. However, I can say that I know without a doubt that the Lord takes what the enemy means for evil and turns it around for good. The Lord has *always* done that in my life even with the most hurtful experiences. *God is faithful.*

> *"But as for you, you meant evil against me; but God*
> *meant it for good,"*
>
> (Genesis 50:20)

One situation that I am able to share involved the death of my mother and our poodle, Mandy. After we moved back to New Mexico in the summer of 2005 and my mother went to be with the Lord in heaven six weeks later, Mandy became extremely ill. She was an adorable, black bundle of love, but when we were in Texas she began to have bladder infections, one after the other.

Three months after my mother died, we took Mandy to the veterinarian and X-rays showed that her tiny bladder was full of bladder stones that looked like jelly beans. We had been praying for her for to be healed for over six months, just as we had prayed for my mother to be healed, but the Lord had not healed Mandy. That day, October 17, we made the deeply painful decision to have her life ended rather than subject her to surgery, recovery, and probable continued problems with her bladder. Mandy was twelve years old. Of course, my husband, daughter, and I all cried profusely as we said, "Good-bye," to our precious friend and family member while the veterinarian gave her the final injection.

I remember telling the veterinarian that my mother had just died three months earlier which was adding to our grief over Mandy. I did not know the complete reality of that statement at the time. I have since learned that pain piggybacks pain and trauma piggybacks trauma. However, I did know what I was feeling and the pain was tremendous.

As time passed, I thought that I was pretty much healed from the grief and pain of losing my mom and Mandy. Much to my surprise, I found out differently in February 2009—*over three years later*! Bob took me to the movies for my birthday. We saw the movie, *Marley and Me*, which is about Marley, a family's dog. Everything was great until the end of the movie. Marley got quite ill and it became clear that surgery would not help him. He was then euthanized with his owner at his side. The family said, "Good-bye," to their beloved pet as they buried him beneath a tree in their front yard.

We had no idea that the plot of the movie would be so close to what we had experienced with Mandy. The Lord knew and He used it to bring about good in my life. As you can imagine, I was crying during those last scenes. I was not just crying though. I was *sobbing uncontrollably* and I could not stop! It continued as we walked through the parking lot to our car and for about fifteen minutes while we sat in the car. Bob could not console me. What the Lord revealed to me was that the grief and pain from losing Mandy had not been totally healed and when it was triggered, pain and grief that I had buried from my mother's death also came up. Bob then began praying for Jesus to release the pain, and as he did, the depth of grief lifted. *Praise the Lord!*

Although this was an incredibly painful experience, I *praise God* that the Lord Jesus has released that pain from my heart and healed me. The opportunity to become angry at God for not supernaturally healing my mother or Mandy was definitely there. By the grace of God, I did not go down that path. I chose to allow the Lord to do the work necessary for my spiritual growth rather than allow the enemy to use the experience for his advantage. After all, they both received the ultimate healing. I firmly believe that I will see my mother and Mandy in heaven after I die. The Lord Jesus has given me great peace regarding that. *Thank You, Jesus!*

This was a good example of how we can know that we need healing for our hearts. When we overreact to a situation or react totally inappropriately, it is usually an indication that some suppressed pain and trauma from the past has been triggered. We have a choice when this happens. We can repeat the same behavior over and over or we can choose to trust and allow the Lord to bring us to a new level of maturity in Him. Our spiritual growth is not a given. It is up to us to pursue it.

If you have survived any type of abuse but have not received the healing and freedom you need from the pain and trauma of that abuse, your spiritual growth will be hindered. I strongly encourage you to seek help from a trained and qualified Christian inner healing minister so that you can walk in the freedom that Jesus died to provide for you. There is a list of suggested resources at the end of this book to help you find someone that can pray with you for healing from the abuse. *Take the step.* Jesus promises that He will be with you.

Chapter Fourteen

Praying with Abuse Survivors

A buse is not a comfortable topic for most Christians but it needs to be addressed. Our spiritual growth includes facing and dealing with things from the past that are keeping us weighed down and unable to fulfill our God-given destiny. That includes abuse of any kind.

The effects of emotional, mental, verbal, physical, sexual, spiritual, and ritual abuse, including satanic ritual abuse, are lurking in the past of many of our brothers- and sisters-in-Christ. The churches are full of people who have been wounded by one or more of those forms of abuse, but they do not know how to receive freedom from the things that torment them in their minds, hearts, and spirits. It is time for the Body of Christ to step up to the task of showing the compassion of Jesus to those within His Body!

> *Blessed be the God and Father of our Lord Jesus Christ, the Father of mercies and God of all comfort, who comforts us in all our tribulation, that we may be able to comfort those who are in any trouble, with the comfort with which we ourselves are comforted by God.*
>
> (2 Corinthians 1:3-4)

Sadly, many abuse survivors have been told by others in the Church to forget the memories, confess the Word of God, and go on with life. That is not comforting to anyone, especially someone who has experienced severe abuse! Many of them have also been told that God "allowed" it to happen, as if they should thank Him and just get over it. God did not *allow* the abuse to happen to them, but He did not prevent it from happening. The word *allow* can imply to abuse survivors that the Lord approved of the abuse and that idea causes the survivor even more pain. It also suggests to them that the abuse was acceptable to God, or that He intended for it to happen.

Our Most High God hates abuse! However, He will not interfere with man's free will. Since Satan is roaming about seeking to kill, steal and destroy, abuse is rampant in the world. God does not sanction or endorse abuse in any way! Rather, our Just and Holy God does not stop man from making wrong, hurtful, and abusive choices that affect others any more than He forces us to love Him and receive Jesus into our lives.

Our Heavenly Father does, however, provide the healing needed from that abuse, emotional pain, and trauma. The lie of the enemy is that God does not care because He did not stop or prevent the abuse from happening. John 3:16 says, "For God so loved the world that He gave His only begotten Son, that whoever believes in Him should not perish but have everlasting life." If God didn't care about us, He would not have provided this opportunity for our salvation. *God loves us and is good all the time!* The devil is bad all the time. *Evil* is contained in devil.

We must get to a level of inner healing within ourselves before we reach out to help others. If we do not obtain freedom from our own past pain and trauma, we can do additional damage with careless and damaging words to those who come to us for help. We must minister from a pure heart of compassion.

God has used the pain and trauma from my past to grow a tremendous amount of compassion in me and a desire to see others set free as I have been set free. As an abuse survivor, I can relate to many of the hurting people who have sat before me in need of healing for deep inner wounds. My experiences are not exactly the same as those of anyone else but they are similar enough to draw my heart to those who have been abused. This connection to the person needing prayer is essential for the ministry to be the most effective. Of course, the Lord can use anyone to help heal someone with deep hurts. He is God and nothing is impossible for Him. However, if you desire to pray with wounded people, ask the Lord to stir your heart to feel what He feels for them. He *will* answer that prayer!

I have prayed with abuse survivors of so many different situations and the common thread is that they all need to be shown the love of Jesus. Seeing an adult man sobbing at our kitchen table because of the horrible emotional and spiritual abuse he had just gone through was enough to cause *righteous anger* and an enormous amount of compassion to rise up in my heart. I, too, have experienced deep pain and trauma at the hands of other Christians. The compassion that filled me allowed me to pray with that man to the best of my ability at the time, and the Lord used me to help comfort one of His children as a result. *Praise the Lord!*

> *"Be angry, and do not sin"*
>
> (Ephesians 4:26)

The above verse would not be in the Bible if it was not possible to be angry and not sin. This describes *righteous anger.* I was filled with righteous anger due to the situation above because the devil had used others in the Body of Christ to bring such severe emotional pain to a loving, follower of Jesus. Righteous anger is an area that many Christians do not completely understand.

Also, most people who have suffered severe abuse and trauma will have anger attached to the pain. Until the pain is released, the anger will be there. Just suggesting that they need to forgive and repent of their anger does not usually give them lasting freedom. *The anger that they are carrying is often justified.* Telling them to repent is further abuse. I have learned that the best way to help a person receive freedom from that anger is to pray for Jesus to release the pain. When the pain from the abuse leaves, spontaneous forgiveness often occurs and the level of anger greatly decreases or disappears all together. *Praise God!*

A few years ago, Bob and I met with a couple who had also experienced emotional and spiritual abuse through other Christians. The wife was carrying a lot of pain and anger from the years of abuse. She asked, "What about those of us who have not been able to go on with our lives?" *This is the problem.* There are too few members of the Body of Christ who know how to pray with other Christians to help them receive healing and freedom. There are also too many who are ready to deny the problem exists or offer some "words of encouragement" that are not comforting at all. We must respond to the need for healing in the Church if the Body of Christ is going to be effective in reaching the lost and sharing the Good News with unbelievers.

I cannot tell you how many women I have prayed with that have been molested or sexually abused in their childhood but *never told anyone.* One such woman, now in her late seventies, was repeatedly molested by her father as a young child. As she told me about the abuse, the tears she shed were from the deep pain and trauma that had been buried for seven decades. She had never been able to tell anyone about the abuse before, but when Jesus brought that pain forward to release it, the healing and freedom that followed was beautiful. The fact that she felt safe enough to share the pain with me was a huge honor. We must *never* forget what a privilege it is to be allowed to witness Jesus healing people's deepest pain and trauma in their hearts!

The Body of Christ must also be released from the practice of criticizing what we do not understand. The person sitting next to you in church may be dying inside and never tell you anything but, "I'm blessed," when you ask how they are doing. One of the ladies that I have prayed with had an exceedingly traumatic past and never had the privilege of a healthy childhood. Sally (not her real name) grew up on the streets with no permanent place to call home.

Sally's life as a child was unimaginable. She went from the "frying pan into the fire" after she was adopted. What should have been a wonderful experience for her turned out to cause her more pain and trauma. Appallingly, her adoptive father sexually molested Sally on a regular basis and also abused her emotionally, mentally, and spiritually. Sally only escaped his abuse by getting married years before she was ready. With her already severely damaged mind, heart, and spirit, her decisions were not the best and her life continued to be filled with pain and trauma.

After Sally accepted Jesus as her Lord and Savior, her life did *not* instantly go from horrific to *heaven on earth*. Many years of abuse and the trauma of absence, not receiving what she needed emotionally, physically, and spiritually growing up, had left their mark on her. When she turned to people in the Church for help, many of them did the best they knew how to help her, but a lack of understanding often resulted in more harm or a lack of help at the very least. I am not blaming the Body of Christ for her condition when she came to me for inner healing prayer. I am just saying that we need to do our best to help abuse survivors, especially those who have turned to the Lord.

Sally is just one example of a woman in the Body of Christ who can be easily misunderstood. *Listen.* We do not know everything about inner healing and the damage that trauma causes to a person's mind, body, heart, and spirit. However, we do know that there are physical consequences from a childhood like Sally's. There are also emotional and spiritual issues that cannot be denied. We must have an increase of compassion for our brothers- and sisters-in-the-Lord. Even though Sally has received much freedom and healing through different forms of prayer ministry, many Christian women like her are suffering the effects of abuse, but they are afraid to reach out for help.

Abuse survivors do not normally share their past history with other Christians for fear of condemnation and gossip resulting from their prayer requests. Too many times, when such prayer requests are shared with other believers, those who are trusted to keep them confidential use them for what is nothing less than pure gossip. We must stop this devastating practice in the Church. Countless women have told me that they have gone to their pastor or someone else in the church for prayer only to find out later that their extremely personal prayer need was broadcast to the whole church or throughout a prayer chain. Confidentiality is not an option if the Body of Christ is going to receive the inner healing so desperately needed.

Many abuse survivors also suffer from Environmental Illness. Having experienced this myself and having received training in this field, I can speak about this with some level of authority. Environmental Illness (E.I.) is real. I was once so ill with E.I. that I had a very large cylinder of oxygen next to my bed. I also brought two small cylinders of oxygen with me when I traveled away from home. Reactive airway disease, not being able to breathe due to a reaction to some environmental element, was not a fun thing to live with. I was treated for the symptoms and effects of the disease, and I eventually improved to the point that I no longer needed oxygen. *Praise the Lord!*

Nevertheless, I do not believe that the Lord created our bodies to react negatively to our environment. We are "fearfully and wonderfully made" (Psalm 139:14). The problem is that abuse takes a huge toll on our bodies and especially on our immune systems.

Therefore, we must address the root cause of the Environmental Illness if we are going to be effective in facilitating true healing in a person's body. Doctors are used mightily by God but many of them admit that they can only do so much. Our bodies were designed to heal but if there is an issue of past trauma that is at the root of the physical illness, it must be dealt with in order for the cycle of illness to be broken. Jesus can reveal the root cause of physical illness but we must ask Him.

> *"Until now you have asked nothing in My name. Ask, and you will receive, that your joy may be full."*
> (John 16:24)

Bob and I have both witnessed physical healings that resulted from people receiving inner healing prayer when we had not prayed for the physical condition to be healed. In fact, several times, the person did not even mention that they had a physical problem until the end of the session *after it was healed.* One such example was a lady who, at the end of her session, exclaimed, "My back pain is gone!" She had been suffering with severe back pain for weeks before her prayer session. After Jesus released her from the pain and trauma of past emotional and sexual abuse, the physical pain also left her body. Weeks later, this woman reported that the pain was still gone. *Praise the Lord!*

This does not always happen as a result of a person receiving freedom from the trauma of past abuse but it does occur quite frequently. Another woman who had arthritis in her neck that made it painful for her to turn her neck to the side also experienced a physical healing after her inner healing prayer session. During her *Healing the Brokenhearted Ministry* session with me, Jesus released an enormous amount of emotional pain that she had been carrying since childhood. After her prayer session, this woman was amazed when she realized that the arthritis pain had left her neck!

This woman was able to experience the release of a large amount of emotional pain in one session. However, we must be particularly sensitive to the abuse survivor's ability to handle the emotions that come forward as a result of inner healing prayer. Some people have a large capacity for emotional pain and others have a very limited capacity. This all depends on the amount and type of trauma they have experienced and how the emotional control center in their brain developed as they were growing up.

Since we do not normally know all of the details regarding a person's past, knowing the Lord's voice and obeying Him is absolutely essential when praying with abuse survivors. People have related experiences to me of being pushed too far by well-meaning prayer ministers. When the Lord says, "It is time to stop," *it is time to stop!* It does not matter what you were hoping to accomplish during that session. The Lord, and only the Lord, knows how much a person can handle without receiving further damage. This is critical when ministering to ritual abuse survivors.

Ritual abuse is a reality. It can occur in Christian and non-Christian groups alike. ***Please do not read the rest of this chapter*** if you feel yourself becoming agitated or feel emotional pain being triggered.

Ritual abuse is an extremely sadistic form of abuse of children and non-consenting adults. It is methodical, systematic sexual, physical, emotional and/or spiritual abuse. Extreme forms include mind control, torture, and highly illegal and immoral activities such as drug use, murder, child pornography and prostitution. The most severe form of ritual abuse is satanic ritual abuse (SRA.)

Ministering to SRA survivors must be done with the utmost of care. Survivors of satanic ritual abuse have been programmed by their abusers to commit suicide if memories of the abuse are accessed. Therefore, I always enter a healing prayer session with an SRA survivor with extensive prayer prior to the session and relying totally on the Lord's direction. We do not dig for memories during a *Healing the Brokenhearted Ministry* session, but we do minister to them if they come forward spontaneously. Again, the Lord Jesus Christ knows how to best bring about healing and freedom for an SRA survivor.

The protocol that my husband and I have setup for our ministry requires that a person must *not* be actively participating in the cult, and that *they* must willingly be seeking freedom from the trauma of satanic ritual abuse. I would never knowingly try to minister to anyone who was currently involved in a satanic cult. The dynamics involved in helping people escape a cult environment are not something that we have been trained to be involved in. Therefore, I have only ministered to survivors, those who are no longer involved in the cult in the physical realm. The spiritual realm is a totally different story.

The challenge in ministering to SRA survivors includes helping them get free from the control of their abusers in the spiritual realm. That can sometimes be a tremendously difficult challenge, and the survivor *must* be in agreement with the prayer ministry for it to be effective. I have had SRA survivors referred to me for prayer by others who have been praying with them only to find out that the SRA survivor was not the one seeking my help. Thankfully, the Lord has directed me not to accept those cases.

A word of warning… If you are considering praying with satanic ritual abuse survivors, be absolutely sure you have intercessors praying for you and your family, the survivor, and the ministry sessions. The spiritual warfare surrounding the freedom process for SRA survivors is over-the-top. We do not need to be afraid, just diligent and wise in preparation and prayer coverage. This type of ministry is not for the faint of heart. You must be able to stand in the battle with the kingdom of darkness. *Thank God*, we are on the winning team!

As I began to pray with SRA survivors, the spiritual warfare against us increased significantly. However, the Lord definitely told my husband and me that it was His timing for this level of prayer ministry to begin. Having the confidence that the Lord would protect us no matter what the enemy sent our way was all we needed to take this huge step. I can say without any hesitation that, although the road has not always been easy for us, *God has always been faithful*.

Sarah (not her real name) suffered satanic ritual abuse as a child. She was *not* a willing participant, and she tried several times to escape from her abusers. Since she was only a child, she was unsuccessful. Today, as an adult woman, she has been escaping from her abusers in the spiritual realm as Jesus Christ has been setting her free from and healing the unimaginable pain and trauma that she experienced so many years ago. It has not been a quick or easy process, and it has required an enormous amount of determination and faith on Sarah's part. The Lord has honored her faith by doing an incredible work of healing within her mind, heart, and spirit. Sarah has said that the *Healing the Brokenhearted Ministry* has been so different from other methods that she tried in order to get healed from the horrific abuse. She told me that she would leave feeling raw and in pain after other attempts at freedom, but that she never felt that way after a *Healing the Brokenhearted Ministry* session. *Praise the Lord!*

After many of the prayer sessions with Sarah, she would send me an email with praise reports from the inner healing that she had received. The following are just two examples of what Jesus Christ did for this precious woman who loves Him beyond description. These are Sarah's own words.

> "I have waited to write this note until I was sure that the peace and joy I have been feeling since Tuesday was really gonna stay with me or not. Well, it is staying with me. *Praise Jesus!* Since Tuesday I have

been able to connect with and draw close to Jesus like I did ten years ago. I feel like something truly broke off of me Tuesday and the *joy* is profound— and it's lasting—that is what I'm so rocked about. Of course, I am breathing in His Life daily or none of it would stick! Anyway, I wanted y'all to know about this amazing shift that Jesus has blessed me with. *Thank you* Kathy, the lady who assisted you, *and Jesus* for helping make freedom more and more of a *reality* for me. I have gotten up off of that stupid mat and now I'm starting to walk—*running comes next! Hallelujah! Thank You, Jesus!"*

A few months and several sessions later, I received this email from Sarah after another powerful *Healing the Brokenhearted Ministry* session.

"I wanted you to know that I am feeling better Kathy! *Praise God!* I feel more stable and calmer than I ever have. I feel hope, life, and good things opening up (somewhere, not sure where, though). Spiritually, I mean. Just a good hopeful feeling that I have inside. I *know* that I know that I know that something is better! I wanted you to know Kathy. Thank you for all of your prayers. You mean so much to me. The lady who assisted you does, too. Kathy, you just know it when your insides go to another level of peace and calm. It's so real! And *so wonderful!* I know there is plenty more work to do though, but I want you to know how blessed and grateful I feel. Jesus is so amazing."

What can possibly compare to fruit like this in our lives for the kingdom of God? Sarah is a totally different person than the one that

I began praying with several years ago. She received enough healing to become involved in ministry herself. Sarah wants to help others because she is so grateful for what the Lord Jesus has done for her, and she is now free to the point of being able to serve the Lord. This is what it is all about and what makes it all worthwhile. *Praise the Lord!*

Chapter Fifteen

Ministry Testimonies

I have already discussed in previous chapters much of my own testimony of healing from the abuse and trauma I experienced in my life. My freedom and healing came in waves or levels through several methods of prayer including my crying out to the Lord in desperation, the intercessory prayers of others, prayers for physical healing, deliverance prayers with trained ministers, and inner healing prayers. The following ministry testimonies are examples of spiritual, emotional, and physical healing that other people have received in which Bob and I have personally been privileged to participate. These testimonies are meant to encourage you and to strengthen your faith that you, too, can receive healing and freedom through Jesus Christ.

> *"And they overcame him by the blood of the Lamb and by the word of their testimony, and they did not love their lives to the death."*
>
> (Revelation 12:11)

The most marvelous testimony of someone asking Jesus Christ to be their Lord and Savior occurred during our trip to Israel in December 2007. Bob and I, as well as two other ladies in our group, were unwinding in the lobby of the hotel one evening after a very long day. We had been playing rummy and about to call it a night when a young man walked up and started talking to us. He asked us if he could watch as we played and we agreed. Richard (not his real name) seemed drawn to us. I want to emphasize that *we did not seek him out in any way.* He just came to us. This was a divine appointment!

Richard was in his teens and had come to the hotel with some friends after the Sabbath celebration at his home. Richard was a Jewish young man and a typical teenager with a slightly know-it-all attitude about everything. After watching us for a few minutes, he asked if he could teach us a new card game. We allowed him to do so as we were all curious where the Lord would take this encounter. As Richard taught us the game, it became apparent that he was very interested in us and the good time we were having without drugs or alcohol. I explained that the Holy Spirit filled us with the joy he was witnessing in us. He was speechless.

Then, I proceeded to talk about Jesus Christ and the fact that we had just walked down the Villa Dolorosa, where Jesus carried the cross on which He was crucified. Richard remarked, "I have never heard this before." There he was, living in Jerusalem, and he had never heard this about Jesus! He wanted to know more. So, we told him more about Jesus, God's Son. We told him that Isaiah 53 described Jesus and asked if we could read it to him. Richard was not familiar with the name *Isaiah* as he always read the Torah in Hebrew, not in English. However, when Bob began reading Isaiah 52 as an introduction to Isaiah 53, Richard immediately recognized the verses in Isaiah 52.

From that point, the Holy Spirit did an incredible work of salvation in this young man's heart. His attitude changed drastically and he said, "Yes," when Bob asked if he wanted to accept Jesus as his personal Lord and Savior. Bob led him in a short prayer and asked if we could pray for the Holy Spirit to fill his heart. Richard agreed. It was the most beautiful example of someone accepting the Lord that I had ever seen, and it happened right there in Jerusalem!

After we prayed with Richard, we explained that *he was still Jewish* and that he did not need to do anything different as far as his normal religious practices were concerned. It was after midnight when we all hugged and cried as we said, "Good-bye," to this precious new follower of Jesus. This truly was the highlight of our trip to Israel.

Salvation—spiritual freedom through Jesus Christ—is definitely the most important form of freedom that anyone can experience. It is freedom that affects our eternity. As a result of God's grace and mercy, emotional healing through Jesus Christ can also be received after that first step is taken. *Praise the Lord!*

During our trip to Mexico in October 2008, we prayed for all three types of healing: salvation, physical healing, and emotional healing. It was remarkable! This trip was very different from the other trips we had previously taken to minister in Mexico. That day, we did not know where we would end up when we crossed the border at Juarez. At that time and ever since, Juarez has been a volatile and extremely violent area. Thousands have been killed as a result of drug cartel wars. In spite of that, we knew that the Lord was asking us to go into Mexico at the Juarez border crossing to minister and give children's shoebox gifts and stuffed animals wherever He directed us to go. It was another step of faith which, as always, turned out to be exceedingly fruitful.

The whole trip was led by the Holy Spirit. We had asked Steve and Rita, the Directors of the *Healing Rooms* in Albuquerque, to go with us since they were fluent in Spanish. After crossing the border with our van full of stuffed animals and shoeboxes containing school supplies and toys, I drove south, and we just kept following the Holy Spirit's instructions. We ended up in a colonia south of the city and saw some women and children walking down the dirt road. A *colonia* is an exceedingly poor neighborhood similar to a slum in the United States but usually much worse. This one did not have any running water, electricity, or indoor plumbing. Those women and children were so blessed when we stopped the van and got out to talk to them. Steve explained that God had sent us there to give the children gifts. We prayed for them in Jesus' name. The smiles and excitement of the children and their moms were priceless!

As we continued to drive around the colonia, we came to a Christian church and the pastor *just happened* to be there. He was a young man who had been building this church to replace a very small building next door that was falling apart. He was immensely proud of his little church building and amazed as we explained that we had come to pray with him and give gifts from the Lord to the children in the colonia.

The pastor's arm had been injured in an accident and was visibly twisted. We asked if we could pray for his arm. As we did, we all saw his arm straighten and he said that the muscle felt stronger. *Praise the Lord!*

Then the pastor went out and gathered about fifty children and a dozen women from the area for us to have a little church service. It began with a message from the Lord through me and Steve. At the end of the message, Steve invited anyone to accept Jesus Christ who did not already know Him in their heart and several children and a few of the women responded. We also gave them Spanish Bibles that we had purchased before the trip.

As we continued to minister, the Lord told me that one of the women had been exceedingly sad for the past several days and that she had even asked God why He had abandoned her. I shared that and also said that the Lord wanted to heal her heart that day if she would come up front for prayer. Steve translated this but none of the ladies responded. I asked Steve to let them know that, even though their friends were there and it was hard to admit they were so sad, Jesus really wanted to take away their sadness. A lady stood up and came to the front with tears streaming down her face. She was overwhelmed with emotional pain, and as I prayed for her that pain turned into joy. She smiled and laughed and gave me a huge hug. *Praise the Lord!*

At the end of the little service, we distributed the stuffed animals and shoeboxes to the children. They were all so well behaved and polite, thanking us as we handed them a gift from Jesus. All the children waited until every child had been given a gift before they opened their boxes. What a blessing it was to see them so grateful for these unexpected gifts from God!

From this colonia, we drove to a second colonia. The pastor's husband from the second colonia had "coincidentally" been visiting the first pastor when we arrived, and he asked if we could come to their church when we were done at the first one. Of course, we agreed and, as we were looking for the second colonia, we drove past a Christian orphanage! This was an answer to prayer because we had hoped to bless children in an orphanage with some of the gifts we had collected from the Body of Christ in New Mexico.

At the second colonia, we were also able to bless the woman pastor with some Women's Bible study materials in Spanish that had been donated for this ministry trip. She was so excited to receive them as she had recently started a Bible study group with women from that colonia. *Wow, God!* Of course, the children from their church and a few others that they gathered from their colonia were also blessed beyond description by the stuffed animals and shoeboxes filled with gifts. We prayed over the children and adults before saying good-bye and heading for the orphanage.

Once we arrived at the orphanage, we were allowed to enter the locked compound after explaining why we had come. There were about a hundred children and a dozen women at the orphanage that afternoon. Some of the children were out for the weekend visiting friends, and we had the exact number of shoeboxes for the ones who remained with a few stuffed animals left over. *Praise the Lord!* The director of the orphanage had been there for about twenty years, and she asked for prayer for strength and energy for her to be able to continue serving the Lord and the children. Those children were obviously well cared for with the limited resources that this modest orphanage was given. What an honor it was to bring surprise blessings to the director, the other adults, and all those precious children!

This Holy Spirit led trip took a total of only four hours after we crossed the border into Mexico. *What an awesome God we serve!* He knew exactly where we needed to go and, as long as we were willing to listen and obey in spite of the danger in the physical realm, His mission was accomplished and He was glorified.

Just a few weeks after returning from this glorious trip to Mexico, Bob and I went to Brazil with Gary and Kathi Oates. While we were there, Kathi was asked to speak at a women's conference of approximately two thousand women. Two other ladies and I accompanied Kathi to that meeting. As Kathi gave her testimony and prayed for those in attendance to receive healing from emotional pain in their hearts, weeping and sobbing filled the auditorium. However, the Holy Spirit miraculously brought the women back to a place of peace before the prayer time was over. That was my first experience personally witnessing the Holy Spirit minister inner healing and freedom from past pain and trauma to such a large number of women at the same time. That experience gave me the faith to later minister similarly to groups.

While I was attending that meeting, Bob was praying for the sick at a different church. *Tumors disappeared in front of his eyes* as he prayed with people and one little girl could not have been more touched by the Lord. Susie (not her real name) was five years old and had a growth on the bottom of one of her feet. As Bob prayed over her foot, the growth completely disappeared. All the pain was gone as well. Susie was ecstatic as she ran around the room. She ran back to Bob's arms and gave him the biggest hug you can imagine. She was grateful beyond words for what the Lord Jesus had done for her!

At another church on the last day of that trip, the Lord told Bob to pray with a man in a wheel chair. The man had a stroke four years earlier and he was completely paralyzed on his left side. He had been bedridden for over two years. As Bob prayed, the man tried to get up, and Bob helped him out of the wheel chair. The man started taking baby steps and then regular steps. He walked about thirty to thirty-five feet, rested, and walked another ten to fifteen feet while Bob helped stabilize him. This man's family was in awe of what they were witnessing. The crowd around him clapped for joy at what Jesus Christ was doing in this man's body. *Praise the Lord!*

Bob and I prayed for and witnessed multiplied dozens of miraculous physical healings in Brazil but the healing that impacted me the most was an emotional and spiritual healing. A young man, Jack (not his real name), came up for prayer during one of the services.

Jack told me with tears running down his face that he was homosexual. He said that he had been through deliverance, counseling, and much prayer ministry, but could not get free from the homosexuality. I asked Jack if he had been sexually molested as a child, and he acknowledged that he had. I then explained to him that when something like that happens, a part of our hearts can carry that pain and, until the pain is released to Jesus, it can be difficult to get free. That was my total explanation to Jack.

Then I asked Jack to close his eyes and focus on Jesus which he did quickly. I asked Jesus to show Jack if there was a part of him that needed to be set free. Jack saw a little boy on the screen of his mind. The little boy was Jack at the age he was when he was molested. *This is very important*—I did *not* suggest any of this to Jack. Everything that he saw and heard came from the Holy Spirit, *not me!*

I asked Jesus to minister to little Jack, and his tears just kept flowing. I encouraged Jack to let the pain and hurt go to Jesus. I continued to pray for several minutes as he released an enormous amount of pain to Jesus.

Next, Jack told me that he believed that the molestation, which occurred numerous times, had happened because he liked it and wanted it to happen. I asked Jesus to speak His truth to Jack about that. Astonished, Jack said, "I did *not* like it and it was *not* my fault!" He had believed that lie for almost twenty years. What freedom he received when Jesus told him the truth!

After Jesus finished ministering to that little boy, Jack saw himself as a slightly older little boy in his mind. This boy had witnessed his father beating his mother many times. He was extremely angry. Jesus ministered to him and released the pain. He was able to receive the love of Jesus.

At the end of this prayer time, I led Jack through a prayer to invite these little ones to be reunited with the rest of his heart. Again, the tears flowed in abundance. Then I asked Jack how he was doing and he said the older boy was still angry. I had asked Jack earlier and he assured me that he had previously forgiven those involved in his abuse including his father. So, I commanded the spirits of anger, violence, and hatred to leave Jack in Jesus' name. When I did that, an overwhelming peace came over Jack, and he later told me that he had *never* felt peace like that before. Those demonic spirits had been attached to the little ones that had come forward. Once Jesus ministered to them, the demons had no legal right to stay, and they left quickly. *Praise the Lord!*

The last thing that I prayed with Jack was for the infilling of the Holy Spirit. When it was all over, Jack was still in tears but they were now happy tears and he gave me a giant hug. This all took about twenty minutes at the altar. These were the very basic steps of the *Healing the Brokenhearted Ministry* which I had been trained to do several months earlier.

However, *I do not advise that this type of ministry be done at the altar under normal circumstances.* It is much better to be in a private place where the ministry recipient can feel safe. Since the Lord arranged for Jack's freedom and healing at that altar, that is where we prayed. I never try to put God in a box and always set aside any preconceived ideas so that the Holy Spirit will have total freedom to minister whenever and wherever He chooses.

Please do not try to do this yourself from my brief description above. There are many things that can occur when the Lord opens up someone's heart during this type of inner healing prayer ministry that you need to be trained to respond to properly. When a ministry recipient is in this vulnerable state, deep pain and trauma can be triggered. Demonic spirits can manifest that have been attached to the pain. *You must be prepared for anything!*

Bob and I also witnessed many people receive physical, spiritual, and/or emotional healing while we were praying in the *Healing Rooms* from 2006 to 2009. One man with whom Bob prayed suffered from an extreme case of diabetes that required him to take three different types of insulin several times daily. After he prayed with the man, Bob had instructed him not to stop taking his medication but to check his blood sugar as he normally would and take his medication as needed. The man continued to monitor his blood sugar levels but noticed they were normal every time that he checked them over a period of days after the prayer session. Several weeks later when the man returned to the *Healing Rooms* for prayer for another issue, he reported that the Lord had healed him! He had not needed to use insulin since Bob and the team prayed with him. *Praise the Lord!*

A lady that came to the *Healing Rooms* for prayer had been diagnosed with spots on her liver. She was scheduled to have surgery. Two other ladies on the prayer team and I prayed with this woman. She felt that she had been healed but I encouraged her to return to her doctor for another test to be sure. I received a card from this woman a few weeks later in which she reported that an MRI showed no cancer anywhere in her body. She did not need the surgery. *Glory to God!*

While Bob and I were praying with people that came to the *Healing Rooms*, we also led *Broken Heart* ministry sessions there. During those sessions, a person would tell us their life's history and as they talked about things, we would pray for healing for the situations that had caused them pain. People received a level of healing and freedom through that ministry. However, one of the things that I repeatedly asked the Lord after several of those sessions was how some of them were able to survive the horrific trauma that they had experienced. When I went to North Carolina in August 2008 for the *Healing the Brokenhearted Ministry* training, that question was answered. I then understood the marvelous way that the Lord had designed us to not only survive traumatic situations, but to continue to function at some level in spite of them.

Since that time, Bob and I have been privileged to witness Jesus heal and set many people free from past pain and trauma through the *Healing the Brokenhearted Ministry*. The following testimonies are from ministry recipients, men and women, who have received freedom and healing through Jesus Christ and the *Healing the Brokenhearted Ministry*. I have changed the names in these testimonies and any identifying information to protect the ministry recipient's privacy.

➤ Susanna reported during her *Healing the Brokenhearted Ministry* session, *"Since Jesus has ministered to the pain connected to my mother, I have been able to remember and think about the good things that happened with my mother. This was a huge improvement."*

➤ Peggy said, *"I am amazed at the difference four sessions has made in my healing from childhood abuse. I can sleep better, not waking with feelings of fear, loneliness, or despair. I feel peace, happiness, and gratitude when spending time alone at home. I am more relaxed, outgoing, speak more, and am letting others emotionally close to me. I have joy and wonder and excitement that the enemy had stolen from me but that Jesus has healed and returned to me."*

➤ Carol reported, *"After my HBH sessions last year, I went to my doctor and told him how much better I was doing and that I did not think I needed the antidepressant that I was taking any more.*

He told me how to wean off it and I did. I have not had the deep episodes of depression that I had been having since. My life and family issues have been very stressful but I am dealing with it all so much better with the Lord Jesus helping me like never before!"

➤ Grace shared, *"I am doing very well and I feel that this last session for Healing the Brokenhearted was especially helpful. I've gone through enough sessions for it to be really effective now. I'm really relieved through the healing from things of the past. Thank you for your service and the other ladies who were working with you. Above all, thanks be to God who helps us to overcome what we've been through and for His healing power. I'm doing fine. Thank you and God bless."*

➤ Heather stated, *"Thank you for loving me in so many ways: in power, deliverance, victory, freedom, tenderness, gentleness, and in steadfast love! I am experiencing such a sweet peace in my heart as it is becoming more and more filled with the precious Spirit of love! May your absolutely beautiful ministry continue to bear God's supernatural fruit!"*

➤ David sent a note that said in part, *"Thank you for facilitating the work of the Holy Spirit; it is making a difference for my family and I. Without your work, my family would be lost... Yesterday was a great day for me! The Holy Spirit was very strong in me and took over my thoughts and actions to facilitate a miracle. The whole family had a very bad attack from the evil one...The miracle for me was that I experienced no feelings of fear, anger, or retaliation—just an inner, unshakable knowledge of what to do. While the storm was raging, I was calm."*

➤ Bob ministered *Healing the Brokenhearted* to Jerome. During his session, a little boy came forward in Jerome's mind that was carrying the pain from being sexually molested by a youth pastor at a church camp twenty-five years before. As Bob prayed, Jesus set Jerome free from pain and trauma. While he was crying, Jerome kept saying, *"You mean that it was **not** my fault and I did **not** want or enjoy it?"* That is what Jesus had spoken to his heart. Jerome left smiling and filled with the joy of the Lord. Bob ministered to him again a few months later and he was still doing fine. Jesus truly had set him free!

➤ Christina reported, *"As a result of my last two sessions, I'm feeling stronger and happier. I have more joy and more freedom in significant areas of my life! Breakthroughs! ...and an assurance that Jesus is right beside me, taking care of me... and I have tools for dealing with the attacks from the enemy... Wow! Thank you, thank you for your ministry. It's a gift from God."*

➤ A message left on our answering machine from a ministry recipient said, *"Hi Kathy and Bob, this is Mary. Just want to let you know Kathy, that session we had yesterday was just totally astounding! I feel totally different—no more dizziness, no more fog. It was just, thank you, thank you! Thank You, Lord, for making the way that I could receive that ministry session. That session was incredible! I just feel one hundred percent different, like night and day. Thank You, Jesus! Thank You, Jesus!"*

➤ Terry wrote a beautiful poem to God, thanking Him, after her first, very powerful session of *Healing the Brokenhearted Ministry*. Jesus had healed her heart in deep areas where she had been carrying pain and trauma for several decades.

➤ I ministered *Healing the Brokenhearted* to Alicia who called her daughter the next day and told her that she had slept through the night. This was the first time in years that she was able to do that! Her family also noticed that Alicia was much less angry and wanted to know what had changed. *Praise the Lord!*

➤ Margaret gave me this testimony after receiving the *Healing the Brokenhearted Ministry*. For two weeks, she had been able to not take the pain medicine that she had been using to help her sleep. She went through some withdrawal, but she had been sleeping well many nights and her head was much clearer. Margaret said that she believed that a good portion of this was due to the ministry she received with me. *Praise the Lord!* She called a few weeks later to say that she was off the pain medicine for sleeping for over a month and she was doing very well. Margaret was involved in other activities and doing much better. **(We *never* tell anyone to stop taking any medication. We *always* refer them to their physician for all medical decisions.)**

➤ Bob ministered two *Healing the Brokenhearted Ministry* sessions to Charles. After the second session, Charles told us that he was doing so much better. *"My friends, family, and people that I work with noticed a difference in me and asked what has happened! I am also sleeping with no problems. As things come up in general, I have been able to handle them better."*

These are just a few of the remarkable testimonies that we have received over the past several years. Bob and I give all the glory and praise to the Lord Jesus Christ for the freedom and healing that these precious followers of Jesus have received. You, too, can receive healing and freedom from past pain and trauma through the loving ministry of Jesus Christ regardless of the severity of the experience. However, you must take the first step and seek help from trained Christian prayer ministers. The Lord Jesus wants to heal you just as much as He wanted to heal those whose testimonies you have read. He does not have favorites. Even the Pharisees knew that Jesus did not show personal favoritism. God loves each one of us and desires the best for us!

> *Then they asked Him, saying, "Teacher, we know that You say and teach rightly, and **You do not show personal favoritism**, but teach the way of God in truth:"*
>
> (Luke 20:21, emphasis added)

Chapter Sixteen

Ongoing Revelation

'Call to Me, and I will answer you, and show you
great and mighty things, which you do not know.'
—Jeremiah 33:3

N o one but God knows everything about healing hearts! He has taught us and many others a lot regarding ministering to the brokenhearted over the years, but we must be careful not to get comfortable with and settle for what we have already learned. We must press in and pray for an increase of revelation from the Lord. There are too many followers of Jesus and soon-to-be followers of Jesus that need their hearts healed.

> *Therefore I also, after I heard of your faith in the Lord*
> *Jesus and your love for all the saints, do not cease*
> *to give thanks for you, making mention of you in my*
> *prayers:* ***that the God of our Lord Jesus Christ, the***
> ***Father of glory, may give to you the spirit of wisdom***
> ***and revelation in the knowledge of Him, the eyes***
> ***of your understanding being enlightened;*** *that you*
> *may know what is the hope of His calling, what are*
> *the riches of the glory of His inheritance in the saints,*
> (Ephesians 1:15-18, emphasis added)

As we seek guidance from the Lord for this Holy Spirit led ministry, we must also keep in mind that Jesus Christ of Nazareth is the One who heals peoples' hearts. I do not minister to the brokenhearted prophetically. What I mean by this is that, although I hear the Lord quite well, I do not lead a ministry session by telling anyone, "Thus says the Lord." When a ministry recipient asks me what I think Jesus meant by something they sensed, I pray and ask Jesus to tell them. I may have an idea of what Jesus meant and, many times what I thought was what He later revealed to them, but I can be wrong. I believe that it is always best for the person to hear or sense something straight from the Lord. They will believe Him and the impact is much greater. The person will remember what Jesus speaks directly to their heart. So, as I pray with those who are carrying pain and trauma, I do so with "fear and trembling."

> *Serve the LORD with fear, and rejoice with trembling.*
> (Psalm 2:11)

Ongoing revelation from the Lord is not a given. The Lord wants to continually reveal more of His character and will to us, but we must spend time listening and waiting on Him. Without an unending and diligent pursuit of God's plan, we will become stagnant and the ministry recipients will receive less than the Lord's best through us. This requires sacrifice on our part. We must lay down our will and be totally submitted to the Lord. *Jesus never said it would be easy* but He said it would be worth it. As I have said before, seeing the fruit that I have seen makes it all worthwhile.

> *The entrance of Your words gives light; it gives understanding to the simple.*
> (Psalm 119:130)

Studying the Word of God is essential in gaining understanding and ongoing revelation from God, the Author of all knowledge and wisdom! We cannot begin to comprehend the depths of the Lord's wisdom but we can and should certainly chase after it to the best of our ability. When we enter the ministry of healing hearts, we are committing to a ministry of great fruit and fulfillment. We are also entering a place in the spiritual realm that *requires* ongoing revelation from the Lord to stay in the race. As Hosea 4:6 says, "My people are destroyed for lack of knowledge." The best way to get the knowledge necessary to serve the Lord in inner healing ministry is directly from His Word and personal time spent with Him.

Learning from others who have already spent time and energy seeking revelation about healing the brokenhearted is also crucial as we set our sights on excellence in serving the Lord and the brokenhearted. I have been diligent about studying what others have gleaned from years of experience in this type of ministry. If you think that you know it all and have "arrived," *think again*. Keep an open heart, mind, and spirit to new revelations in this area. However, always follow the warning in the Bible to test the spirits. Make sure that what is being taught lines up with the Word of God. Anything revealed by the Holy Spirit will *always* glorify God!

Beloved, do not believe every spirit, but test the spirits, whether they are of God; because many false prophets have gone out into the world.

(1 John 4:1)

"However, when He, the Spirit of truth, has come, He will guide you into all truth; for He will not speak on His own authority, but whatever He hears He will speak; and He will tell you things to come. He

will glorify Me, for He will take of what is Mine and declare it to you."

(John 16:13-14)

The ministry recipients are also an invaluable source of ongoing revelation regarding inner healing. As you pray with people from enormously varied backgrounds of emotional pain and trauma, you will observe the Lord healing and setting them free in countless ways. What works with one person may or may not help another. Only the Lord knows what each individual needs to receive the freedom that only He can provide. We have the privilege and honor of not only participating in their inner healing as prayer ministers but also as students of the Lord Jesus Christ, the best Teacher in existence. *Praise the Lord!*

I cannot stress enough the importance of seeking the Lord's ongoing revelation as you pray with those who have been emotionally and spiritually wounded. Brokenhearted men, women, and children need a safe place to receive the healing and freedom that is promised to them by the Lord. Although Jesus is able to instantly and miraculously release past pain and trauma from a person's heart, mind and spirit, He also uses human vessels to bring this to pass. I encourage you to prayerfully and seriously seek the Lord's wisdom and guidance if you are considering becoming involved in inner healing ministry. It must be a calling from the Lord that you know, that you know, *that you know* is God's will for you. Once you know, be at peace!

"Peace I leave with you, My peace I give to you; not as the world gives do I give to you. Let not your heart be troubled, neither let it be afraid."

(John 14:27)

Remember, the ministry of healing hearts is an extremely important part of the ministry that Jesus Christ brought to this earth.

He loves us so much that—not only does He want us to receive His free gift of salvation and forgiveness of our sins so that we can spend eternity in heaven with the Father—He desires us to be free from pain and trauma. Then we can more effectively fulfill our God-given destiny on this earth. Jesus decreed this in the synagogue as recorded in Luke 4:18, where He quoted the following Scripture from Isaiah 61. Jesus also said in John 14:12, "He who believes in Me, the works that I do he will do also." Therefore, the ministry of healing hearts is a vital part of the ministry that Jesus Christ has passed to us!

> *"The Spirit of the Lord GOD is upon Me, because the LORD has anointed Me to preach good tidings to the poor;* ***He has sent Me to heal the brokenhearted, to proclaim liberty to the captives, and the opening of the prison to those who are bound;"***
>
> (Isaiah 61:1, emphasis added)

If the Lord is leading or has already led you into inner healing ministry, you have been blessed with a priceless gift and the authority to do awesome things for the Lord. Yes, the enemy will fight you tooth and nail, but *Jesus will be by your side every step of the way.* Just be sure your steps are directed by His loving hand. You will witness marvelous healings of wounded hearts as He sets the captives free, and you will see people's lives changed in absolutely miraculous ways!

> *"Most assuredly, I say to you, he who believes in Me, the works that I do he will do also; and greater works than these he will do, because I go to My Father."*
>
> (John 14:12)

Now may the God of peace who brought up our Lord Jesus from the dead, that great Shepherd of the sheep, through the blood of the everlasting covenant, make you complete in every good work to do His will, working in you what is well pleasing in His sight, through Jesus Christ, to whom be glory forever and ever. Amen.

(Hebrews 13:20-21)

Thank You, Jesus!

Suggested Resources

Banks, Bill and Sue. *Breaking Unhealthy Soul-Ties.* Kirkwood, MO: Impact Christian Books, 1999.

Hawkins, Diane. *Restoration in Christ Ministries.* http://www.rcm-usa.org

Khouri, Ed. http://www.thrivingrecovery.org

Kylstra, Chester & Betsy. *Restoring the Foundations.* http://www.rtfi.org

Leaf, Dr. Caroline. *Who Switched Off My Brain.* Dallas, TX: Switch on Your Brain USA Inc., 2008. http://drleaf.com

Oates, Kathi. *Open My Heart, Lord.* Moravian Falls, NC: Open Heaven Publications, 2006. http://kathioates.com

Shelton, Bob and Kathy. *All for Jesus Ministries.* The *Healing the Brokenhearted Ministry* blog. http://allforjesusmin.blogspot.com/ E-mail address: allforjesusmin@comcast.net

Smith, Eddie and Alice. *Spiritual Housecleaning.* Ventura, CA: Regal From Gospel Light, 2003.

*And we know that all things
work together for good to those who love God,
to those who are the called according
to His purpose.*

—Romans 8:28